FOLLOW THE THUNDER

JASON DOZELL

FOLLOW THE THUNDER

WITH
STUART WATSON

pitch

First published by Pitch Publishing, 2024

Pitch Publishing
9 Donnington Park,
85 Birdham Road,
Chichester, West Sussex,
PO20 7AJ
www.pitchpublishing.co.uk
info@pitchpublishing.co.uk

A CIP catalogue record is available for this book
from the British Library.

ISBN 978 1 80150 919 0

MIX
Paper | Supporting responsible forestry
FSC® C013604

Printed and bound in the UK on FSC® certified paper in line
with our continuing commitment to ethical business practices,
sustainability and the environment.

Typesetting and origination by Pitch Publishing
Printed and bound by CPI Group (UK) Ltd, Croydon, CR0 4YY

Contents

For Dion, Andre and Emile –
I'm in awe of the men you've
grown to be.

Foreword by Terry Butcher

MY FIRST memories of Jason Dozzell are that he was very shy and very wary. You could see he was in awe of everybody.

I could certainly relate to that. Like him, I'd grown up an Ipswich Town supporter, watching from the terraces. Like him, I joined the club as a teenager, albeit a slightly older one, and was soon playing alongside my heroes.

In the same way Jason looked up to us, I'd looked up to the likes of Kevin Beattie, Allan Hunter, John Wark, Mick Mills, Trevor Whymark, Clive Woods and Bryan Hamilton before they all suddenly became my team-mates.

I can tell you now, that's the weirdest thing in the world. You have to motivate yourself to keep moving and keep playing in the training sessions because all you want to do is just stop and watch them. People don't understand how difficult it is when you're playing against legends and you've got to try and tackle them, kick them and make them look like idiots.

Which of those guys looked after me? Well, Big Al used to put his arm around me, but sometimes it was more of a headlock because he was telling me to be more aggressive!

So when Jason first burst on the scene as a 16-year-old I knew exactly what he was feeling. I guess I always felt like an older brother looking out for him.

It was wonderful to be a part of his historic debut goal in '84. In some ways it was bittersweet. I was delighted for him, but I was also wondering how it might affect him. Sometimes you see kids break into the first team and they get arrogant and cocky and start to strut about. I wouldn't have a lot of time for people like that, but I had a lot of time for Jason because he was never 'Billy Big Time'.

We all knew that he wasn't going to be just a flash in the pan. We had seen from the very first training session that he was a real talent. This kid had a lovely touch and great control. He was a languid mover, didn't have blistering pace, but his brain was very sharp and he got into good positions.

He still apologises to me for his role in our Milk Cup semi-final defeat to that lot up the road in '85, bless him. To be honest, I was more angry at the fact Russell Osman had been left in the stands. Russell would have sorted Steve Bruce out!

I smashed up the changing rooms at Carrow Road that night. If there was one thing I hated hearing it was the sound of Norwich players celebrating a win over Town. I know Jason has the same strength of feeling about them too. How was he on derby day? He used to go mad; he'd say five words in the changing room instead of one! Honestly, he was like a mouse.

When he got on the pitch, though, he was different. He wanted the ball, he wanted to do his job. It was like a flick of a switch. He was well coached by Bobby Ferguson, but it was very natural to him as well. He used to drift in behind people, get the ball, turn and use it. The physical side he could do too. He was quite tall and muscular, good in the air. A bit like with Trevor Whymark, you'd think he'd left his coat hanger in his shirt when he went on the pitch because he had such big shoulders.

You'd hear opponents shouting at each other to mark him. A centre-half would get dragged out into nosebleed territory, then Jason would pop it off quick and move again. Sometimes he'd get absolutely smashed. Defenders wanted to hurt him because he was a danger, but he could take it. He was a real joy to play with.

I know Jason has spoken in this book about getting sucked into the game's drinking culture at a young age. Us older players can probably take much of the blame for that. It's true, sometimes we'd go bananas if we didn't have a game for a few days. That's what happened in those days though – you worked hard and played hard. It helped bond us together as a group.

It was really nice coaching alongside Jason in the Ipswich academy further down the line. I'm glad he's still doing some work with the club's Foundation because he does a great job. I saw one day he was coaching a young striker and he'd set up an exercise for front-post finishing that had real attention to detail. That's how he got a lot of his goals. He didn't really smash a lot of balls. He generally passed it into the net, a bit like Warky used to.

Whenever I see Jason now we talk about the old days and he is very, very modest. He needs to remind himself that he's among the top ten goalscorers and top ten appearance-makers in Ipswich Town history and spent a long time playing in the

Premier League. There are very few people who can say that. I think some people underestimate the career he had. I always say to him, 'We haven't done too bad as Suffolk boys.'

Ipswich Town Football Club is our medicine. It can heal. Whenever I go into Portman Road the hairs on the back of my neck stand up because I've been there as a fan, I've been there as a player and I've been there as a coach. There's no better place in the world. I know Jason feels the same.

Where he's been mentally in recent years has not been a nice place. I'm proud of him for speaking so openly about that. It's been lovely to see how far he has come from such a low moment in his life. To me, it feels like he's come full circle. To me, it feels like he's the real Jason Dozzell again.

He's one of our own and, at his core, he's a lovely, lovely guy. I hope, after reading this book, you get a sense of that.

Foreword by Kieron Dyer

I'M 11 years younger than Jason Dozzell. When I joined Ipswich Town at the age of ten, in 1989, he was the club's rising star and soon became my football hero.

I lived on the next street along from Jason. His mum knew my mum and one day, when I was about 13 or 14, they arranged for him to turn up at the house and surprise me. He probably won't remember that moment, but it was a big deal for me. When I opened the door, I pretended to faint!

I loved that title-winning team of '92. The following season they took the Premier League by storm for a spell. When we beat Manchester United, Jason had a prime Paul Ince chasing shadows. I was completely in awe.

It broke my heart when he subsequently moved to Tottenham. I was in the crowd the day he came back to Portman Road and I hated hearing some of the stick he got. I was in that corner where he ran off and did that stupid celebration. I wasn't brave enough to clap him, but I did think 'fair play'. That's the only time in my life, other than when I played against Ipswich for Newcastle, that I've wanted Ipswich to concede a goal. That's how much of a hero he was to me.

This might sound arrogant to say, but from the moment I started training with the Ipswich first team at 16 until the day I left I always believed that I was the best player at the club. The only time I didn't feel that way was when Jason came back for his second spell in '97. Then I thought I was the second-best player. His brain was so quick and his technical ability was top. He wasn't even at the peak of his powers then, either.

We had a great connection on the field during that brief time playing together. I only ever had that with one other Ipswich Town player and that was Jim Magilton. That was down to their football IQ. Those sorts of players, who always think two or three steps ahead, are very rare.

When Jason got let go by George Burley it was rumoured that people inside the club thought Jason was a terrible influence on me. I don't know if that was the reason, but if it was then it makes me sad because it couldn't be further from the truth. Jason was a great role model and always gave great advice. It's just a pity I didn't heed his words when it came to what not to do off the pitch!

For some reason, I think the team that won promotion via the play-offs in 2000 is loved a lot more than the team that won the title in '92. That pains me a little bit. No disrespect to the likes of Matt Holland and Marcus Stewart, because they are legends of the club, but, for me, Jason is the biggest legend in Ipswich Town history since the Bobby Robson era.

With the ability he had, you can probably say he underachieved in his career. But I'm sure when we read this book, we'll understand more why he didn't quite hit the heights he looked destined to.

Back then, there was no one to guide you like there is in today's game. All of a sudden you go from really poor to really wealthy. I found that hard in a city like Newcastle, so I can't imagine what it would have been like for Jason in the bright lights of London. I opened up about my past and how that affected me in my book. I'm intrigued to read about Jason's deeper emotional story and how that affected his career.

I just hope this club legend gets the love that he deserves.

1
What's That Noise?

SATURDAY, 9 December 1967. The nation was still feeling the afterglow of Bobby Moore lifting the Jules Rimet Trophy at Wembley when I entered the world. That World Cup triumph was masterminded by a manager, Sir Alf Ramsey, who had been forged in Ipswich. It's the town I was born in and one I'm immensely proud to have always called home.

It's often said that I grew up a goal kick away from Portman Road. Not quite, but almost. The distance between 67 Elliott Street to the home of Ipswich Town is 500 yards – a straight walk through Alderman Road Rec. I heard the stadium before I ever saw it, though.

At five years old I was already allowed to mess about on the street in front of our house. First, I'd hear these strange rumblings. *That's weird.* Then, out of nowhere, an almighty roar would vibrate off the streets and echo around that small residential area. It was so loud the neighbours' windows would rattle.

I'd stop still, frightened, frozen to the spot. *Is that thunder? Maybe it's a lion or a bear just around the corner?* My young mind would race with wild thoughts.

This went on for weeks. I'd forget all about that burst of noise, be back in my own little imaginary world, kicking a stone or swinging a stick, and then freeze with fright all over again as the sudden sound reverberated off the concrete. Eventually I ran inside one day and asked, 'Mummy, what's that sound?' 'That's the football,' she told me with a smile. *Football?* That answer brought a mixture of relief and curiosity.

It wasn't long before that noise provided a thrill rather than a fright. I followed that thunder. Ridiculously, little more than a decade later, I was the one creating it.

* * *

It was just me, my mum and my older sister Charletta, or 'Tootie' as we call her, in that house.

I'd call it very humble beginnings. Two up, two down. No inside toilet. I wouldn't say we struggled, we just didn't have much. The furthest we'd go on holiday was to Clacton on the Essex coast. We always had loads of presents at Christmas, but I do remember going to the cupboard and often seeing just bread and ketchup. Veg? What's that? With my mum it was fish fingers and chips most nights. Bless her, she did the best she could.

Mum is the number one person in my life and always will be. I don't know everything about her life before me, but the little I do know doesn't paint a pretty picture. I've always assumed she doesn't really want to talk about it, because it's never really been brought up, and that tells me a story in itself. It's not a topic I've really pushed and it's still not one I'm really keen to explore too deeply, to be honest.

All I know is she had five other kids before Tootie and I came along and they were placed in the Dr Barnardo's children's care home at Harland House, 15 miles away in the seaside town of Felixstowe. I can only imagine how difficult life must have been for my mum. She must have felt completely overwhelmed. Rightly or wrongly, she made that decision. All I can say is that I guess she did what she felt she had to do at the time.

Why didn't Tootie and I get put into care too? Was that ever close to happening? I don't know. I can only guess that our dad, who wasn't their dad, had something to do with it. Some people need answers to questions like that, whereas I've never gone looking for them. You'll soon see that's been a theme in my life.

My five oldest siblings – Kenny, Tony, Cheryl, Carolyn and Nathan – weren't complete strangers to Tootie and me growing up. We knew who they were and they'd come into our lives sporadically through the years with the odd visit to Ipswich. I think they got brought up with more structure than we did. They were on the beach every day, got regular meals and eventually left care as adolescents to make their own way in the world. Mentally it was tougher for them growing up though. We were with our mum and they weren't. It's difficult to put myself in their shoes.

There have been issues. At times, I think, they've found it hard to accept why my mum did what she did. Once we all became adults it could get awkward and get political. We'd go to BBQs together, have a drink and things would come up. We've all got older though, had children and grandchildren of our own, and the last 20 years, thankfully, has been the strongest and most stable we've ever been. Everyone gets on with my mum now, but that's not always been the case. It could have been a lot worse.

I'll talk more about some of my wider family, and my dad, as this book goes on, but for now I'll focus on those early years of seclusion.

Tootie is a year and a bit older than me. We were very close growing up and still are today. That bond, which will never be broken, was probably strengthened by the fact there was no extended family to go to when we were kids. There were no weekends with a roast at the grandparents' or anything like that. All that was fine by me. I didn't know any different and it gave me more time to play football. There was definitely more good than bad in my childhood.

I have to respect what mum did as a single mother. She didn't get everything right, but she's got the heart and decency of any good human being. She's kind and loving, but she had her struggles and would get frustrated. Her mood swings were up and down.

Everyone who knows Francine Dozzell will tell you she's a real character. She knew a lot of people, put it that way. I remember she had this radio scanner thing, God knows where she got it from, which meant she could listen in on the police. Where they were going, who they were after – she could hear it all. As news of a raid crackled over the airwaves she would frantically ring people and shout, 'Get out of there quick!' The next day someone would knock on the door with a bunch of flowers in hand. 'Cheers Fran, thanks for that!'

She could be hard. I'd often suffer the wrath of the slipper. That came into full force the one time I got in trouble with the police as a kid. My mate Gino Washington and I were walking to the train station along Ranelagh Road to go and watch Ipswich play away. We could only have been eight or nine and, chances are, neither of us had eaten any breakfast before rushing out the door.

These were the days when you could ask the milkman to leave a few extra groceries on your doorstep. Gino spied some Jaffa Cakes outside one house. He looked at me, I looked back at him. Within a flash he'd grabbed them and started legging it. I had no option but to join the getaway. Were the police called or did they happen to just be driving by? I don't know, but all of a sudden we were being taken to the station.

Mum came to collect me. *Uh oh.* I knew I was in trouble. Pleading that I was guilty by association did not wash. I tried to catch her eye the entire walk home but she just stared straight ahead. I needed a plan because I knew full well she was going to switch as soon as we got in. The second that front door opened I took those stairs three at a time as she gave chase, then I jumped into bed and covered myself with the blanket. I wasn't stupid. That extra layer killed the pain a bit as she whacked away. Parents were a lot stricter then than they are today.

Mum could be really fun too. When I was 16 she got a job as a lollipop lady – I'd love to know how she passed the interview for that with no relevant experience – and was assigned a crossing near our house on London Road, the main route out of the town.

I'd just got into the Ipswich Town first team. As a fresh-faced young pro, my focus should have been on earning the acceptance of senior team-mates and the next day's big away game as we hit the road on the team coach. Instead, all I could think about was surviving that nightmare first bit of the journey.

Mum, who knew exactly what time we were setting off from Portman Road, would calculate when we would reach her crossing and step out on to the road to greet me. In turn, I had to perfectly time a ten-second slide down into my seat, pretending to look for something on the floor, as she stood in the middle of the road jumping up and down, waving frantically and looking for me through the windows. All the lads would look up from their game of cards and be nudging each other, going, 'Look at this nutty lady!' That went on for ages. Every single trip. 'Here she is again!' the lads would all shout. They all thought it was hilarious.

Eventually Mum, ignoring pleas to stop cramping my style, started stopping Trevor Kirton's bus. Knock, knock. Doors open. 'Tell Jason good luck!' she'd cheerfully call up the stairs. I wanted the ground to open up and swallow me. Embarrassed in front of all my heroes. I was absolutely mortified. She was just proud of her little boy, though.

Tootie was quite happy playing with her doll's house for hours on end as a kid. For me, the house could get a bit claustrophobic. I had no real boundaries and would be out until ten o'clock every night from a very young age. Football was my sanctuary.

Elliott Street and the surrounding roads were very vibrant, very diverse. I had freedom and loads of friends. There was

Eamonn Kelly, Rodney Tricker, David and Grant Burroughs, Gary De'Ath, Pasquale Iachetta, who I'm still best mates with now, and many more.

We'd play curbsies and posty. The rules of posty were simple: one touch, hit the lamp-post and you stay in. Strike that lamp-post at just the right angle and the ball could end up all the way down the road. So many windows would get smashed before we all ran off. We were all little rascals around that area. Not bad kids, just little scallywags.

During the school holidays we'd all go over to Portman Road to watch the first-team players train on the practice pitch where the astroturf is now. A chance to watch my heroes, yes, but there was an added motivation. I wanted to get my hands on a football.

I had a plan. Professionals don't shoot over a fence that high, I knew that, but on a rare occasion I'd seen the ball hit the top of the crossbar hard and be diverted up and out into the road. I had to be ready for that. Patience was the key. I'd wait all day if I had to.

When that moment finally arrived, I'd keep my eyes on the prize, like a wicketkeeper in cricket, and snaffle it straight under my top before the other four or five kids could react. Before the players and staff had finished their shouts of 'oi, get back here!' I was gone. In '81, when those iconic adidas Tango balls came out, I'd wait and wait for hours to get my hands on one of those.

After a while the staff started to cotton on, so I had to try and disguise myself a bit, putting on a hat and loitering by different parts of the fence. That was the Elliott Street mentality – you get what you can and face the consequences if you're caught.

It was a sheltered life. I wasn't really learning anything. I was just stuck. Go out, play football, come home. No holidays, no visiting other family. That's probably why I became so good at football. That was all I had.

My football education came on Alderman Park Rec, just behind the North Stand. Everyone from the area would congregate there, all ages, and there'd always be enough for 11-a-side. The big boys picked the teams. I wasn't too flash. It wasn't my style to go out there and try to be the top boy. If I nutmegged someone or tried to go past someone with a stepover I don't think that would have gone down too well. I didn't want people to get the hump with me, so I just got it and passed it on. I kept my game pretty simple.

That meant I learned receiving skills. I always gave myself three options – can you pass back, can you go sideways, can you go forwards? Being on the half turn, rather than facing one way and not knowing what's coming behind you, was a form of protection. That way I couldn't get kicked. When they realised they couldn't kick me, they started to drop off. Then, recognising that I was being afforded extra time and space, I started having more than one touch and trying different things. They didn't know what to do with me. It was all development.

The first bit became my game really. Awareness, always on the half turn, one-touch passing. Nowadays, in academies, that's all they teach. But that was a self-taught skill for me and I think it enabled me to think for myself more when I did become a professional.

It wasn't just on the rec that we played. Carl and Steve David, who I'm still good friends with today, lived just the other side of London Road on Surrey Road. They had a concrete area near their house that everyone played five-a-side on – we all called it 'The Dump'. There was a little car park area we played on too. It was quite territorial. The 13- and 14-years-olds ran it and us seven- and eight-year-olds had to patiently wait our turn to stage a game or, on the odd occasion, be asked to join in to make up the numbers.

Some of the best footballers in the world learned the game on the streets. The South Americans are a prime example of that. In England we had Wayne Rooney. Those sorts of players are just wired differently. They're mentally strong because they were left on their own to fight. From a young age you learn through trial and error. I think I got a bit of that.

I went to Westbridge Primary School on the Old London Road from the age of three to six. I was meant to be there longer, but when my sister moved school I was a mess – Mum says I was just crying all the time – so in the end I got transferred to Ranelagh Road to be with her. I loved that school. It had a little outdoor swimming pool and a lovely concrete playground with a pitch marked out and goals at either end.

That's all I needed. Happy days.

That was a diverse school with lots of different nationalities. I don't think many of us were destined for Oxford or Cambridge, but we had loads of good athletes and at the annual Inter Schools' Sports Day held at Sprites Lane we'd always clean up. I was captain and won the 100m and

200m. Our girls did pretty good too. I remember us coming back on the bus celebrating with the cup.

It was football I was obsessed with, though. As well as playing for the school, I played for the 7th Boys' Brigade on Kelly Road. We won a competition and Ipswich midfielder Brian Talbot gave us the trophy. That was two bits of silverware in quick succession. That first bit of success tasted sweet and I craved more.

After that I had a choice whether to go to Stoke Park or Chantry High School. My best friend, Pasquale, he went to Stoke Park, but my mum said I was going to Chantry. I was gutted. There were more tears over that.

No father figure, a mum having her struggles, no extended family, no real boundaries, hanging about with my scallywag mates and showing little interest in school. It's easy to come to the conclusion that had I not made it in football I might have fallen in with the wrong crowd and gone down a bad route. I really don't think I was that way inclined, though, to be honest.

Academically I wasn't interested, but I wasn't a troublemaker either. I was painfully quiet, observing, just trying to work things out. Socially I was rubbish because I'd not really developed those skills.

It wasn't an unhappy childhood at all. I'm just not sure it prepared me particularly well for what was ahead.

2

Put Your Hat Back On!

'What is a football club in any case? Not the buildings or the directors or the people who are paid to represent it. It's not the television contracts, get-out clauses, marketing departments or executive boxes. It's the noise, the passion, the feeling of belonging, the pride in your city. It's a small boy clambering up stadium steps for the very first time, gripping his father's hand, gawping at that hallowed stretch of turf beneath him and, without being able to do a thing about it, falling in love.'

THE LATE, great Sir Bobby Robson really summed up football fandom in his 2008 book *Newcastle – My Kind of Toon*, didn't he? That wide-eyed, instant, helpless addiction to the game was exactly how it had been with me and Ipswich Town when Bobby was in charge, just without the father to hold my hand.

I can't remember exactly what my first Ipswich Town game was, but it would have been when I was six or seven during the 1974/75 season. They opened the gates at half-time in those days and all us kids from round the area would pile into the West Stand for the second half. You'd just sit where you could.

I vividly remember being at the FA Cup quarter-final against Leeds in March 1975. That match still holds the record for the biggest home crowd in the club's history. There was 38,010 officially packed into Portman Road that day – though there's every chance it was more – and I squeezed on the pitch behind the billboards. It finished 0-0 but I was mesmerised. The following weekend at Portman Road it finished Ipswich 5 Newcastle 4, with Bryan Hamilton grabbing a hat-trick. Now I was truly hooked. That lifelong love affair had well and truly started.

Robson's men eventually beat Leeds in a third replay, at Filbert Street (Leicester City's ground at the time), before losing to West Ham in a semi-final replay, this time at Stamford Bridge. I listened to that game on the radio and cried my eyes out at the full-time whistle. From a very early age it was clear how football was going to affect me emotionally. Results would really alter my mood.

At that age I didn't appreciate what I was watching. I was a seven-year-old boy. My mind wandered. I liked to mess about. There used to be this big unused scoreboard in the corner between the West Stand and the North Stand, the type you see at cricket clubs, and, when I got a bit bored, I used to climb up the scaffolding and get in behind it. I'd watch the action peering through the slits around the little blank squares that hung down off pegs and, after a while, I got brave enough to start changing them to the numbered squares that were lying around in that dusty enclosed space. I'd put Ipswich 50, the opposition nil. It always got a laugh from the fans nearby.

The first game that really sticks in my mind, in terms of the actual action, is the 7-0 home win against West Brom in November '76. Four goals for Trevor Whymark and one each for John Wark, Paul Mariner and Kevin Beattie. Mum soon realised how much I loved it and started taking me to a few away games. I remember she took four or five of us boys to Liverpool on the train when we were really little. My older brother Tony, who I'll tell you more about in the next chapter, took me to some games too. I remember him taking me to Tottenham, just me and him, at a really young age. Little did I know then what that particular fixture would mean for the two of us years down the line.

Ipswich Town, the team on my doorstep, secured top-flight finishes of third, sixth and third in my first three seasons of being a fan. Incredibly, the best was yet to come.

Come 1977/78 I was at every game, home and away. Sometimes Mum would take me and sometimes I'd go with Tony. Often I'd just go with a mate. Two ten-year-olds, no parents, getting on the supporters' coach to travel halfway across the country. There's no way that would happen these days, but it was different back then.

I went to every game in the run to the '78 FA Cup Final – Cardiff, Bristol Rovers in the snow, Millwall in the quarter-finals. That was an experience at the old Den. We won 6-1 and there was a riot when our fifth goal went in. Their fans went absolutely ballistic and the game got stopped. All I was thinking about that day was whether my brother Tony, normally in the midst of things when it all kicked off, was all right. Now we were in the semi-finals of the FA Cup! West

Brom were the opposition at Highbury. I'll never forget that train journey into London. There were thousands of Ipswich fans, all singing and making an incredible noise. As a young kid that felt deafening. We won 3-1 and it was a joyous trip back. What an unbelievable performance that was. Next stop Wembley. It didn't seem real.

In the following weeks there was a competition across Suffolk's primary schools to see who could write the best poem about Ipswich getting to the FA Cup Final. Me and my mate Pasquale won it, with our entry printed in the *Ipswich Evening Star*. I was made up. This was around the time I was winning sports days and football tournaments. It felt like everything I touched turned to gold!

We queued up for hours to get those FA Cup tickets. When the big day came, the whole family got dressed up. I wore white trousers, a white top and a big white hat with huge blue rosettes pinned to it. With my Ipswich scarf and blue wristband on, I was ready for Wembley. Me and my mate Eamonn went on the coach. Mum packed us up a lunch and waved us off. I remember getting off outside the ground and within seconds a couple of Arsenal scallywags kicked me up the arse and ran off laughing. The sight of the famous Twin Towers soon got me over that, though.

Saturday, 6 May 1978 remains, after the birth of my kids, of course, one of the best days of my life. I was in the bottom tier and remember looking up and seeing Tony and all his friends in the best seats in the house, front row of the top tier. How they got those tickets I don't know. Maybe they just muscled their way in. I don't know, but I do remember wishing

I was up there too. If you look back at the telly coverage you actually see a little clip of them. There's afros everywhere!

Talking of afros, mine got me into trouble that day. We were like sardines packed in. No one could move. As I said, I was wearing this big hat covered in rosettes and I was quite tall. This guy behind kept moaning at me 'take your hat off', but once I took it off my big afro popped out and obscured his view even more. He burst out laughing and went, 'For fuck's sake, put your hat back on!'

It was a roasting hot day. The atmosphere was just electric. Arsenal striker Malcolm Macdonald was a huge player at that time – he had been scoring goals for fun over the previous few seasons – but Allan Hunter and Kevin Beattie had him in their pockets. Clive Woods was unbelievable on the wing, Johnny Wark hit the post twice, Paul Mariner hit the bar, Roger Osborne eventually got the winner and promptly fainted in the most one-sided 1-0 win you'll ever see. We were just brilliant.

Coming back on the coach everyone was beeping their horns on the motorway. There were flags hanging from bridges and scarves twirling out of car windows. Then I was in among the sea of people outside the Town Hall for the team's welcome home reception the next day.

Having finished 18th in that cup-final season, the league form picked up again. We finished sixth in '79 and third in '80. I was 12 years old as the historic 1980/81 season started.

During the week I'd be over at the practice pitch next to Portman Road. Waiting for a rogue ball to come over the fence, yes, but primarily a starry-eyed kid watching my heroes train. As they walked out I'd shout their names. 'Butcher!'

'Osman!' 'Thijssen!' My heart would skip a beat if I got a little wave back. I was completely in awe. It's stupid things you get fixated with as a kid. To me, Russell Osman looked a million dollars. Long blond hair, body ripped to shreds and socks down around his ankles because his calves were so big. He had the best cars too and a real swagger about him. I looked at my little skinny legs and started doing loads of calf exercises because of him.

I remember a game against Tottenham and a collision between Russell and Graham Roberts, a player who had a reputation for being a hard case. A corner came in, there was a clash and Roberts came off worse. I spoke to Russell about that recently and he remembered it. He said Graham had done Mich d'Avray off the ball and it was a bit of retribution. It's weird the things that stick in your head.

I loved Frans Thijssen. He was stylish and got himself out of tight areas. If I was really pressed to name my favourite at that time it would have been him. But my song was for the man who scored for fun. I'd be in the bath on a Saturday lunchtime singing, 'He's here, he's there, he's every fucking where, he's Johnny Wark!' That would spark a shout from downstairs. 'Stop swearing!' Whatever Mum, I'd think, with pre-teen attitude, before carrying on (with the volume turned down a notch).

The reason I was in the bath at midday was because of the traumatic start to weekends that Mum always used to put me through. I had lovely curly hair when I was young, but Mum insisted on taking me to Adam and Eve's hairdressers every Saturday morning to get it blow dried. I'm black, so you can imagine what that did to my hair. If there was a 100-miles-an-hour wind it would not move. I looked like a black Fonz. Remember him? Fonzarelli from *Happy Days*? Heyyyy! Cunningham!

Everyone else my colour had a nice little afro and that's what I wanted. The guy would be brushing it back and I'd see my mum behind me in the mirror enthusiastically holding two thumbs up. She's beaming ear-to-ear thinking it looks great. 'Do you want a lollipop, kid?' the barber would ask when the torturous process was finally all over. My stony face and crossed arms suggested in no uncertain terms that the answer to that question was no. I was absolutely raging.

I'd quickly have to pull myself together though because the next part of my Saturday was to go and play for South Suffolk. I'd score a couple for them, race home and get straight in that bath. I couldn't go to Portman Road looking like that. I'd mess all my hair up, wash the rubbish out of it and get some Jheri curl in it. Then it was time to get dressed and walk down to the match.

I didn't watch the football for 90 minutes. No. I was a big crowd watcher. I'd never seen life outside of Suffolk, so I was just intrigued by it all. The hairstyles of people from up north were different. I was fascinated by what they wore. To start with the stereotypical football fan was a skinhead in braces and Airwair boots. Then, for some reason, it all changed within a year and going to football started becoming a fashion show. Pringle, Lacoste, Sergio Tacchini – in came all this smart, branded sportswear. From what I gather, it started with the Scousers coming back with these new outfits from

European games and it soon filtered through. I loved it. I thought, 'Wow, I need to get some of that.' Eventually I found a place that sold it – Mick McNeil's on Tacket Street. Mick was a former Middlesbrough and Ipswich defender who'd played a handful of times for England and started a successful chain of sports shops after retirement. It took me a while to save up, but eventually I got myself a Pringle jumper and pair of Stan Smith trainers. After that I was bowling to the games thinking I was a big man.

Out on Alderman Road Rec I tried to mirror Paul Mariner's hold-up play, twist and turn on the edge of the box like Eric Gates, run at people like Alan Brazil, replicate that trademark Arnold Mühren pass, cross like George Burley, attack the ball like Terry Butcher, lead like Mick Mills and be hard as nails like Russell Osman. I'd even dive around in goal pretending to be Paul Cooper. I tried to be all of them in one. I was constantly imitating my heroes.

Oh God, they were the days. Walking to the ground I'd see away fans streaming off their coaches and be thinking, 'How many are we going to beat you by today?' We were that good. I'd be the first one in the ground just counting everyone in, soaking up every bit of the atmosphere and carefully studying the warm-up leading up to kick-off.

European nights under the lights were magical. Aris Salonika, Bohemians Prague, Widzew Łódź, Saint-Étienne, FC Cologne – I think I got more nervous and excited for those games than I ever did subsequently playing myself. I was inside Portman Road for the first leg of the final when we beat AZ Alkmaar 3-0. I then watched the second leg on the telly. They mounted a comeback, but the damage had been done. Ipswich Town, 5-4 winners on aggregate, lifted that magnificent-looking UEFA Cup. Incredible.

We could and should have won the treble that season too. Beattie broke his arm in the FA Cup semi-final against Manchester City at Villa Park. Paul Power's free kick was the difference. That was heartbreaking. We beat Aston Villa three times that season but they pipped us to the title after our hectic schedule caught up with us. It was a travesty we didn't win more really. Still, we were European champions and there's not many that can say that.

In '78, I'd struggled for a view of the Town Hall balcony from down in the crowd. This time, aged 13, I had a plan. Getting there early, I went up Lloyds Avenue to get around the back of where Boots is now. I clambered up a ladder, dragged myself on to the roof and got myself a great high vantage point of the celebrations. One leg hanging either side of a wall, I was petrified of falling. It was dangerous, but it was worth it.

Supporting a football team in your adolescent years really is the most magical time. The noise, the colour, the emotion – everything is intensified at that age. You're learning about the world. Everything is new. For me to get all that when my hometown club was so good – I was blessed.

If anyone had said to me, 'In three years' time you'll be out there playing with those superstars,' I'd have told them they needed locking up. It was unrealistic. I was only 13. I was miles away from that level. Or so I thought.

3
Are You Tony's Boy?

IF YOU live in Ipswich, chances are you've seen or heard of my older brother Tony Swallow.

A 6ft 3in, red-haired black guy. There aren't many of them around. He grew up in a children's home, stood out like a sore thumb and had to fight to fit in – literally. People will challenge you when you look like that, and he certainly likes a challenge. If you want some trouble, you will get it.

Tony's nine years older than me. It became clear to me very early on that he was a well-respected figure in the town and on the terraces. He was big, strong and could handle himself. I was totally in awe of him in the early days.

Everyone would say to me, 'Are you Tony's boy?' I had no father figure. I was maybe looking for something. A sense of belonging. He used to leave me a fiver on the side, things like that. I was thinking, 'Is this the guy that's meant to look after me?'

Tony and his mates congregated in the snooker hall most days and I would join them in the school holidays. They played for money and there was always a lot of tension in the air. All of a sudden, things would escalate and cues would be drawn. Ten-year-old me would be left diving for cover, listening in on the Jamaican 'yardy' insults being thrown around. I didn't know what some of those words meant to start with, but I soon figured it out. The next argument and scrap would never be far away.

I've always been the type of character that's drawn to things that are a little bit different, a little bit exciting, so even without Tony I'd have probably ended up in the North Stand. But my desire to be near him meant I was in there sooner than I should have been. I made the transition at 12, for the UEFA Cup-winning season, and saw a little bit of stuff I probably shouldn't have seen at that age.

I didn't know what I was walking into. This was 1980 when hooliganism was at its peak. In those days they caged the North Stand off – we had three-quarters of the stand and the away supporters had the other quarter. We were penned in like animals.

Back then there wasn't the ID checks like there are now and every game you'd get around 15 or 20 away fans buying tickets in the home section just to cause trouble. You'd be watching the game and after about 20 minutes they'd let themselves be known. A chant of 'Chelsea!' or 'Arsenal!' would go up and then it would all kick off. A few would stand up and fight, while a panic would set in among the rest. People would try and move away from the scene of the trouble. You'd soon start to feel the crush. I was tall for my age and could keep my balance. I learned how to keep my feet high and ride the wave. I'd be on someone's back hanging on for dear life, thinking, 'If I go under, I'm dead.' I'd start somewhere in the middle of the stand and end up right down the front, winded. It was bedlam. Absolute carnage.

I could see the look of fear on people's faces around me. Was I scared? No. Should I have been? Probably. The atmosphere was electric and intense though and I was fascinated watching it all unfold. I made sure I was never right in the thick of it.

The biggest narrative in England 1981, without doubt, was racial tension. In January, there was the New Cross house fire when 13 young black people died at a house party in London. A 'Black People's Day of Action' was organised after that, with 20,000 people marching through London and carrying placards that said things like '13 Dead, Nothing Said'. Two subsequent inquests both recorded open verdicts. Come the March, former Conservative MP Enoch Powell, who had criticised the rates of immigration into the UK as part of his infamous 'Rivers of Blood' speech years earlier, predicted a 'racial civil war'. In April, there were the Brixton riots as black youths clashed with the police over increased use of stop-and-search.

Amid a recession, unemployment passed the 2.5 million mark for the first time in nearly 50 years. Under Thatcher's government there were a lot of frustrated and angry young men. A lot of them used to go to football to let off some steam.

I wouldn't call Tony a football hooligan. He was just fiercely loyal to Ipswich and wasn't the sort to back down. Because of the way he looked, he got targeted. The away fans would come here and pinpoint him. When I got in the North Stand, I couldn't believe what I saw. The insults flying back and forth were incredible and most of them were aimed at my brother and all his black mates. It was nigger this, nigger that. That was hard for me to see and hear.

To be honest, you couldn't really call what happened in the stands fighting. It was so tightly packed that no one could get any punches out. Inside the ground it was all shoving and pushing. Outside the ground was when the fists flew. The away supporters at Portman Road would get let out by the park. What they'd do is walk up Alderman Road, turn right and come back down to get around the police cordon and get to the Ipswich fans.

Tony and the boys were Ipswich through and through. Every club has got that element of people who will do anything to defend their football club. It's tribal. People aren't going to come to our place and take the piss. I'm not condoning it, but that was the attitude. Obviously, they'd then try and make their mark on other teams' patches, marching straight into a home team's main pub ahead of kick-off. We're not talking a handful of people here by the way, we're talking hundreds. It would be like cowboys and Indians in the street.

I can't remember how old I was when Tony took me to Norwich for the first time, but I know I was young; certainly far too young to be involved in what I saw that day. We went up in a Transit van and it wasn't long before I heard talk of stopping at a pub. 'Great, a nice burger and chips,' I thought naively. Food, however, was not on the agenda. Before I'd even had a chance to get to the front doors, I could see through the windows that the chairs were flying. It wasn't long before Tony and his mates came running back out, I was bundled into the van and we were pulling out of the car park, tyres screeching.

Outside the ground things intensified. One of our group went ahead as a scout and shouted back, 'They're over here!' With that, Tony charged off like a bull to reach the targets. That happened several times over.

I was relieved when we got inside the ground. 'Phew, I'm safe here,' I thought. Then the game kicked off, I looked around and clocked there weren't many blue scarves around us. It turned out we were in the River End, the home stand. Seeing that moment of realisation on my face, Tone turned to me and just said, 'Don't worry boy, you'll be all right.'

There were about 20 or 30 Ipswich fans in our undercover group and about midway through the first half they let themselves be known. All hell broke loose. I remember us being hauled out of the stand by police, on to the side of the pitch and marched around the perimeter to be shoved in with the away fans up the Barclay end. As we made that walk there were coins and bottles raining down on us. Finally, we got back in the Ipswich pen.

That day was the first time I saw intensity turn into real hate. Ipswich–Norwich just brings something out in people. They overstep the mark.

Tony's reputation grew and grew. Opposition supporters would shout, 'Where's your ginger nigger?' 'Tone, you're going to have to dye that hair,' I kept telling him. One time he did. He turned up for football with all this black dye down the side of his face. For an hour and a half I was glad he'd done it, because he was less of a target, but deep down I thought,

'That's not my Tony.' No one said anything, but he knew. That soon stopped.

My brother was hardcore. You'd think a fight had died down and then a shout would go up of 'there's more over there' and he'd be just running through people to get on the scene first. He'd always come out on top too. I guess he must have got hurt at some point, because you can't win them all, but I never saw it. I do remember once, when I was little, him coming home from a game against West Ham in a yellow adidas T-shirt covered in boot marks.

Did I ever get involved in all that? No chance! I'm not a fighter. I was a shy, reserved kid who played one-touch football so as not to get kicked. I didn't need to be told twice to 'stay back' and 'wait over there'. I'd run to keep up with the action, weaving through the crowd, but always stay 80 yards back once the fighting started.

I can't lie though, it was all a thrill. You couldn't get me out of that North Stand until the day I started playing.

4

Super Sundays

IPSWICH TO Tottenham wasn't the first big transfer of my career. No. That came in the summer of 1980.

By the age of 12, I had already moved clubs twice. First, I went from Chantry Grasshoppers to near rivals New Park Rangers. After that, I switched to Ringshall in Needham Market. It wasn't long, however, before I swapped mid-Suffolk for north Essex.

Ringshall faced Langham Lions in the Under-12s East Anglian Cup Final. Langham had been sweeping everyone aside for a few years, but we got the better of them that day. Their manager got the hump and soon tapped me up. I'm really glad he did too.

Roy Knightsbridge was this big, muscly guy who ran bricklaying gangs and competed nationally as a powerlifter. He was old-school. A man with strong principles, but a real heart of gold.

From day one, Roy made it clear how he expected us to behave and play. Rule one was no swearing and no arguing with the ref. 'He won't win or lose you the game – that's down to you.' Rule two was that we always tried to play the game the right way. 'The biggest sin in football is giving the ball away and the next biggest sin is not supporting the player on the ball,' was his mantra. Rule three was that we worked hard. 'There's no point being better than the other team if you get tired in the last 20 minutes,' he'd say. In the summer, there was lots of running, skipping and lifting weights in a fairly basic local gym. It created a winning machine.

Our parents got given a code of conduct too. Roy told them politely but firmly what he expected from them on the touchlines. I was used to my mum being lively on the sides. She'd always be shouting at me, 'Come on, Jason! You're better than that!' More often than not that would drive me downwards. Thankfully, she respected Roy, saw how the other parents behaved and followed suit. Don't get me wrong, she still had her moments, but in general she became less of a negative influence on matchdays.

Without me knowing it at the time, Roy became a bit of a father figure for me.

I found meeting new people a big deal. As I said, it was just me, my mum and my sister growing up. Because of that I was always a bit wary when new adults came into my life. Roy sensed that vulnerability and let me come out of my shell at my own speed. He knew times were hard for me.

On Wednesday nights he'd arrange for his mate Ray, who worked in Ipswich, to pick me up and take me down the A12 to training. Then, on matchdays, he'd make the 40-minute round trip to come and get me himself.

These days when kids talk about 'Super Sunday' they are referring to settling down on the sofa to watch Manchester United versus Liverpool followed by Arsenal v Spurs. My 'Super Sunday' went like this: Roy would come and pick me up, we'd have a chat in the car, I'd score a few goals for Langham and then we'd go back to his house. That place in the Essex countryside was like a mansion to me. It had iron gates out front and a pool table inside that I'd play on for hours.

Roy's wife would then appear with a KFC and that would be devoured in about ten seconds flat. Eventually, Roy would drive me home and slip me £20 – a lot of money in those days – which would help fund my new North Stand clobber from Mick McNeil's. Those days remain some of the happiest in my life.

Roy's in his eighties now. I went to see him at his home in the quiet Suffolk village of Holbrook recently to reminisce.

'Langham's only a small village and my boy Ian wanted to play in a team,' he explained, when I asked him about how the Lions came into being.

'So I went to all the little outlying villages, knocking on doors and asking if they had any boys aged eight that were keen on football. I told them I was holding trials on Saturday and around 40 kids turned up that I whittled down to about 17 or 18.

'I didn't want anyone helping me train them. I wanted to do it all myself because otherwise you get conflicts of opinion. I worked those lads hard, but made it fun too. They became like my extended family.

'Within a couple of years we'd started to build a reputation. I remember Dick Graham – you know, the Colchester manager when they beat Leeds in the FA Cup [in 1971] – coming to watch one of our games with Brian Owen. He came over afterwards, shook my hand and said, "I can't believe what I've just seen! How do you train these boys?" He was really interested.

'Stuart Slater came to us at the age of ten from Woodall United after his dad phoned me up and said, "I love the way your boys play football." Then I got you, Jason, after that cup final. You made the hairs on the back of my neck stand on end, I tell you. I can still picture you hitting the bar from about 40 yards out. I frickin' couldn't believe how good you were.

'It was your mum who approached me about you joining actually. She said you loved the way we played and wanted to be part of it. I was quite friendly with the Ringshall manager at the time, so I spoke to him and it was agreed you'd join us at the end of the season.

'Your addition just took us to new heights. You and Stuart were just pure footballers who combined so well in the middle. Stuart was only little, so he used to drop back a bit to get the ball then you'd do your thing further forwards. I'd just let you play. It was wonderful.'

I honestly don't remember asking to join Langham. Maybe Mum saw an opportunity for me there. Maybe Roy just saw an opportunity to strengthen his side. It doesn't matter. I loved playing in that team.

Stuart Slater, who was from Sudbury, went on to have a great career at West Ham, Celtic and Ipswich. The two of us in centre midfield, as Roy says, tore it up. Bobby Mayes was on the left – he was a really good player who got into West Ham's academy. Darren Armin, whose son Albie was recently in Ipswich's academy, was so quick on the right.

We were so dominant. Roy showed me the stats that he's still got in a little book. From under-tens through to under-15s, Langham lost just three league games. In 196 matches, they scored 1,170 goals. From under-12s onwards, I contributed a fair chunk of those. I'd always be bitterly disappointed if I didn't get a hat-trick.

'One game we were 3-0 up and you hadn't scored,' Roy reminded me with a smile. 'My mate said, "Jas hasn't got one yet," and I told him, "You watch, he'll have one in a minute." Sure enough you picked the ball up about 40 yards out, went around four players, round the goalie, and rolled it in. On your day you were unstoppable.'

It's true, sometimes I did find it too easy. There was a reason for that though.

* * *

I hit my growth spurt a lot sooner than the other kids my age. It started at ten or 11 and by the age of 12 I was the height I am now – 6ft 2in. Team-mates and opponents were coming up to my belly button. I look back at the pictures now and it seems comical, but it didn't feel funny at the time.

I had to start taking my birth certificate to every game I played because parents would always be questioning my eligibility. That gave me a real complex. On top of that, I wasn't the same colour as everyone else and a few people had started pointing that out. To be honest I felt like a bit of a freak.

All those thoughts disappeared when I had the ball at my feet though. I'd just be running through people, swiping them away and shooting from everywhere to score. I was in a man's body playing against boys. The problem is you can get into some bad habits when you're that much bigger. I knew I could have a bad touch and still regain the ball.

'I'm going to tell you something that I've never told you before because you're tough enough to take it now,' said Roy, as we waited for the kettle to boil.

'In your first season with us, a West Ham scout called Ron Gale phoned me and said he had heard we had a good team and was coming to watch. He mentioned your name.

'It was an East Anglian Cup game. We won. Afterwards I said to Martin Bennett, our skipper, "Did you see that West Ham scout?" He said, "Yeah, but he's gone, he said he wasn't that interested and that he's going to East Bergholt to see an under-16s game." So I went straight down to East Bergholt, didn't I? I pulled up in the little car park, saw a bloke sat in his car and went and tapped on the window. It could have been anyone, but I took my chance. "Excuse me, you're not the West Ham scout, are you?" "Yeah, I am, who are you?" "I'm Roy Knightsbridge from Langham Lions." We shook hands.

'I said to him, "Sorry I missed you, but you were busy talking to the ref." Then, probably because he was feeling a little guilty about that, he went, "I shouldn't do this really, but I'll tell you what I wrote about Jason," and he showed me his notepad. It said something along the lines of "lackadaisical, didn't look interested at times". I can't remember all of it, but it was not complimentary. I said to him, "You're making a big mistake, you probably haven't seen the best of him today, but he's frickin' unreal."

'Sensing my passion, he told me that as soon as we faced a London team in the Met Cup to give him a ring and then gave me his card. A few weeks later we had a game at Dagenham who, I think, were unbeaten at the time, so I rang him up. True to his word, he turned up with some other scouts and, of course, we ripped them apart. I can remember their manager shouting at his players, "Wake up Dagenham, these are no country bumpkins!" It finished 5-2, you got two and I think Slater got one. Now West Ham were all over you both.'

That West Ham scout's concerns about my physicality masking some deficiencies were probably valid. It wasn't long before the other boys caught up with me height wise and that's when I had to call upon the muscle memories of my early Alderman Park Rec days. It had to become all about touch and awareness again.

I played up an age group for Suffolk and those county games were a higher standard. We faced Essex when I was 13 and I came up against this big brute of a lad called Tony Adams. He was loud, he was strong and I got absolutely nothing out of him. You could see what a leader he was going to be. We got smashed that day and my eyes were fully opened to the task ahead.

'I knew you was going to make it – no two ways about it,' Roy says, with a proud glint in his eye. 'I don't know if you remember this, but we sat in the car outside your house one night and I told you that you had two choices. One, you can put everything into football and you'll go all the way and have a lifestyle you can currently only dream of, or two, you can get a job. It's up to you.'

I do remember that conversation. Roy brought me out of my shell, believed in me and made me determined to show everyone I could play. I'll never forget what he did for me.

* * *

As a postscript to this chapter, Stuart Slater did join West Ham as a kid. Like me, Ipswich was his team – him and his dad used to have a season ticket at Portman Road – but he felt the opportunity to go to the Hammers was too big. I, as you're about to find out, was prepared to wait a little longer for my beloved Town to take an interest.

It was a shame that Stuart signed for Ipswich just a few weeks after I left for Tottenham in '93. It would have been good to have become his team-mate again in senior football.

'I actually wrote to Ossie Ardiles and told him about how you and Stuart had combined for me and that it would be lovely to get them back together,' revealed Roy. 'He wrote back and said, "I know all about Stuart Slater, I'd love to get him but my hands are tied."

'I had an immense sense of pride seeing your careers take off. You'd leave me tickets at Portman Road one week and then Stuart would sort tickets at Upton Park the next. It wasn't just you two, either. It was great seeing all you boys take on what you'd learned with Langham into adulthood. Bob Mayes went to West Ham too. Martin Bennett, I believe, got offered terms at Watford but went to university. Gary Dutch went to Southend. What a special team you were.'

5

A Tug of War

I'LL NEVER forget my 14th birthday. Picture the scene. It's a Wednesday afternoon in early December and I've not long got home from school, discarded my bag and raced upstairs. Then, suddenly, I hear a commotion outside our front door.

'This is a private property, you're not coming in!' I hear my mum say, in a raised voice. Pressed down low against my bedroom wall, I slowly peeped up through a small gap in the curtains to sheepishly take a look at the altercation unfolding down below. I knew I was the cause of this drama.

This was at our house on London Road, one of the busiest in Ipswich, and the stop-start flow of commuter traffic crawling past was getting quite the show. Some of them were probably listening to the number one song of the day, 'Don't You Want Me' by the Human League. How ironic given the tug of war I found myself at the centre of.

Finally, my head-in-the-clouds way of dealing with the world of professional football had come to the boil.

* * *

Back then clubs didn't have the academy setups they do now, scooping up all the talented kids at the age of seven or eight out of fear of missing out on the next big thing. No, in those days they had Centres of Excellence and you could only sign schoolboy forms with them at the age of 14.

Up until that point you played for your school on a Saturday – representing the district or county side if you were good enough – followed by your local club on a Sunday. For me that was Ipswich & South Suffolk and Langham Lions.

That's not to say clubs didn't scout for young talent from further afield. They did. Just look at the Ipswich glory years teams. John Wark, George Burley and Alan Brazil all came down from Scotland, Kevin Beattie and David Geddis were from Carlisle, Mick Mills came up from Portsmouth, while Eric Gates was from Durham. All of them arrived at Portman Road in their late teens during the '60s and '70s.

Because of Bobby Robson, Ipswich had a big network in the north-east. Players would come down in busloads from Newcastle over the holidays and they would all get put up at Westerfield House. Sometimes though you can end up missing players that are right under your nose. That's nearly what happened with me.

Just as Ipswich eyes looked further afield, scouts from all over the country were venturing into Suffolk territory to see if they could be the first to find the next Roger Osborne or Brian Talbot.

Nottingham Forest were the first club to spot me when I was captaining the Ranelagh Road Primary School team at the age of 11. I still have no idea how that came about. I've also got no real memory of how I attended those trials in the East Midlands. Someone from the club must have taken me to and fro during the school holidays I guess. I do remember meeting Brian Clough. He came into the changing rooms one day and said 'good luck' to us all. I also remember someone from the *Ipswich Evening Star* coming to the house to talk to me about it afterwards and there being a double-page spread in the paper.

To be honest, the magnitude of that all went over my head a little bit. Forest were the newly crowned top-flight champions. All that went through my mind though was, 'Oh, you want me to come and play football? OK. What time are you picking me up?' I'd go there, play, come back and soon be down the park with my mates again.

That September I moved up to high school. My growth spurt kicked in. I moved to Langham and started banging the goals in. Soon I was on the radar of other professional clubs.

The West Ham interest, as Roy outlined in the previous chapter, came about because I was playing my club football in Essex. Again, I went there in the school holidays. That was a real eye-opener for me. I wasn't the big fish in the small pond any more. A lad my age by the name of Paul Ince was immense. I wasn't swatting him aside, put it that way.

Around the same time, Luton Town arrived on the scene. I'm told one of their scouts saw me playing for Ipswich & South Suffolk on a Saturday morning. They were a promotion-pushing Second Division side then under the management of a young David Pleat. I went to those trials with another Ipswich lad, Ian Brown. Browny went on to play professionally for

Birmingham, Bristol City and Northampton, as well as several non-league clubs across Suffolk and Essex.

Luton liked me so much that they put me in with the youth team for a day – a 13-year-old up against 18-year-olds. It was a case of 'let's see what you've got'. Mitchell Thomas, who went on to play for Luton and Tottenham, was a few years older than me and I remember him coming and giving me a little pep talk, which was nice.

So now I'm 13 and I've got three top-drawer clubs interested in me. But, as I said, my brain was not wired to take in the magnitude of it all. I didn't really know what was going on, to be honest. There was no dad guiding me through the process. Anyway, what I was really waiting for was Ipswich Town to come to the party. Thankfully, the chance to really catch their eye finally arrived.

Suffolk made the quarter-final of a national competition and we were drawn against Leeds (I don't know why they competed as Leeds, not Yorkshire, but they did). The game, it was announced, would be played at Portman Road. I couldn't believe I was playing on that pitch. Whenever the ball was out of play, I kept looking up to where I usually stood in the North Stand and smiling. My senses were sharpened. I played out of my skin and scored twice in a 2-2 draw. We played again at a neutral ground, that game ended in another draw, then went up to Elland Road and got beat 1-0 in extra time.

At last, I was on Ipswich's radar. Obviously there was now only going to be one winner in this tug of war. Did I think to tell the other interested parties that, though? Of course I didn't. That's why they all collided on the doorstep on my 14th birthday. They all thought they were signing me. Well, that was my recollection, anyway.

For a more accurate version of events I needed to speak to Tony Dable. Tony was my head of PE at Chantry High School who became chairman of Ipswich & South Suffolk Schools and eventually Suffolk Schools. He'd seen me play a lot and was a real cheerleader of mine. He was also the one who had to step in when things got messy.

First of all, I asked him about why he thought the Ipswich interest came so late and I got a familiar answer.

'Ron Gray was the scout and, for a while, they weren't that interested in you,' he told me. 'I think they felt you were doing everything on physical strength, not ability.

'It was in that Leeds game when I think that view changed. I can vividly remember the ball coming to you around waist height, you stretching out your right foot and, with the outside of the boot, guiding it straight into the path of the left-winger on the break.'

Then Tony told me something I didn't know.

'Luton had already signed you though,' he explained. 'Your mum had counter-signed the forms and you'd have signed it too. That was against the rules, of course, but everyone used to do it. Get the signatures, file the paperwork in a top drawer, then on the 14th birthday out those forms came. It was common practice.'

Mum had signed it, had she? There's a shock. I probably just scribbled my name on something I knew nothing about. Thankfully, knowing how much I wanted to go to Ipswich, Tony intervened. He called up Luton and demanded the forms were returned, which they duly were.

So what happened next? I know Tony was the man who had to act as bouncer during that commotion on 9 December 1981 as my mum and I hid inside.

'I remember that like it was yesterday,' said Tony with a wry smile. 'The school secretary came and found me during the afternoon and said, "There are two scouts from Luton Town here, the head wants you to deal with it." So I went and saw them and they told me, "We want to see Jason Dozzell, we want him to sign."

'I found out what lesson you were in, knocked on the door, went in and asked your teacher, "Can I have a word with Jason, please?" You came out. I said, "Jay, there are two scouts from Luton here, they want you to sign." "No, I want to sign for Ipswich," you insisted. I knew that would be the answer. So I went back to the scouts. "Sorry, Jason doesn't want to sign for Luton, he wants to sign for Ipswich." Off they went. I thought that would be that.

'School ended and it wasn't long before I got a phone call from your mum. "I've got two scouts from Luton Town here, can you come over?" When I arrived at the house they were stood at the gates. One clocked me and made a sarcy comment. "Unlucky teacher, it's outside of school hours now."

'Your mum let me in, leaving them outside, and you reiterated that you only wanted to sign for Ipswich. Hearing that, your mum said, "Well if that's the case they can bugger off," and so I went out and told them politely, once again, that you weren't going to sign.

'As we shook hands, this guy clutched tightly, dragged me in towards him and whispered under his breath, "You fucking bastard." I was shocked. I didn't realise that sort of thing happened. Looking back, I'm glad I helped you get over that hurdle given what you went on to do for Ipswich.'

There you go. In my mind it had been three scouts from West Ham, Forest and Luton respectively all gathered on my front doorstep that day. It turns out it was just two blokes from Luton. The strength of their interest was flattering. Luton were a club on the rise at that time. But I was a mad Ipswich fan and they were the only club I wanted to sign for.

I love my mum to bits, but for her to sign that pre-contract was naughty. Knowing her, I wouldn't be surprised if there had been a backhander involved! Clubs still tap up parents these days. There are rules to prevent it, but it happens. Trust me. What would have happened to me had I come through in this era? Would my mum have had her head turned by serious sweeteners and tried to persuade me that it was best to go elsewhere? Possibly.

To be honest, in my mind I'd decided that if I was going to anyone other than Ipswich it would be West Ham. It wasn't too far away and my Langham team-mates Bob Mayes and Stuart Slater were there. Maybe they weren't interested though.

I've certainly got a lot to thank Tony for. Things worked out all right for him after that incident too.

'It was the way I dealt with that incident that led to Bobby Ferguson offering me a role doing some youth scouting at the club,' he explains. 'I did that until 1989, then John Duncan offered me a full-time job as youth development officer.

'I took a cut in salary from teaching and helped bring the likes of Kieron Dyer, Titus Bramble, Richard Wright and James Scowcroft to the club. There was also the likes of Adam Tanner, Wayne Brown, Leo Cotterill, Kevin Ellis and Richard Logan. I think, in total, there were about 13 or 14 players that we brought in that made it to the first team. And it was you, Jason, that started it all for me.'

Looking back, I get goosebumps thinking about that sliding doors moment.

6

Making Micky Mad

I SIGNED my schoolboy forms at Ipswich sat next to Bobby Robson. He said he'd seen me play for Suffolk and that he rated me. That was a big moment. Completely surreal. This is the manager who has just led the team I fanatically support to two pieces of major silverware.

But again, with little old me, it all went over my head a bit. *OK, this is happening now.* Quiet, reserved, head down, just keep playing football – that was me all the way through to 16. It was probably a good thing. If I had overthought things that could have scrambled my head.

Seven months later, Bobby Robson got the England job. So, by the time I went into the building full-time Bobby Ferguson had stepped up as first-team manager. I wish I'd had Bobby Robson as a manager, I really, really do. But, saying that, would he have given me my debut at 16? I doubt it. I probably wouldn't be in the history books had he not gone. I'm getting ahead of myself though. First, let me explain how I got to that point.

After signing at 14 it was just one training session a week, for two hours, on a Thursday night. My coach was Allan

Hunter who, remember, I idolised because of the '78 FA Cup Final when he had Malcolm Macdonald in his pocket. Big Al took no prisoners on the pitch and didn't suffer fools gladly off it. It didn't take long for me to be on the end of the sharpness of his tongue.

This was less than a year after the Falklands War, which I'd paid no attention to as a football-obsessed kid. Argentina? That was Mario Kempes to me. I loved watching him at the '78 World Cup, so much so that the only football shirt I owned was an Argentina one. Naively, one day I wore it to training and Allan went nuts. He barked at me in that gruff Northern Irish voice, 'Why the fuck have you got that shirt on for? Take it off!' I didn't understand. It was the only football shirt I had and he was giving me a hard time. I was soon educated. I love that guy. We still laugh about that to this day.

By this point, people were really catching up with me physically. I no longer had the height and strength advantage that I used to have. I must have been doing something right though because things happened really fast over the next few months.

Aged 15, they put me in the youth team. I was so proud to be playing two years up in that side, but I was nervous about how I would do. Playing for them, as a schoolboy, was huge for me. Then a couple of months went by, I'd only played a handful of games for the youth team, and I got called up for the reserves. Wow. That was *really* huge.

I scored on my reserves debut, a 3-1 home win against Crystal Palace. That was October '83. I was still only 15. A small report on that game says Bobby Ferguson had delayed his trip to Blackburn to watch. I didn't know that at the time.

The following month, still 15, I was told that I was starting for the reserves against Chelsea at Stamford Bridge. We got there and immediately one name jumped off their team sheet – Micky Droy. Along with Ron 'Chopper' Harris, Micky had a legendary hard-man reputation. These were the days when football's hard nuts didn't mess about. The fouls they dished out you wouldn't get away with now. Studs raked down the back of your Achilles. Waist-high tackles. Nasty stuff. I'd seen what he could do on the pitch with my own eyes.

Brian Owen was the reserve-team coach. He was old-school, hard, wouldn't let you slack off. I looked at him and thought, 'What have I done to deserve this?' It felt more like a punishment than a reward. I may have been 6ft 2in, but I weighed about nine stone dripping wet. There was nothing to me. In the tunnel I was looking across at these man mountains thinking, 'I'm in trouble here.'

That's when the old Alderman Park Rec survival instincts kicked in again. The order of the day was to play one touch. Early on the ball got rapped into me, I flicked it off and quickly got on the move. Keep playing like this, I told myself, and they can't kick you. I could hear Micky grunting with frustration. Increasingly, I could see the veins popping out of his head. He really wanted to smash me, but couldn't. I was having a good game, everything was coming off, then, with ten minutes to go, a cross came into the box and I side-footed in the equaliser. The game finished 1-1.

Bobby Ferguson had been in the stand watching again. He came down to the dressing room afterwards and, with an understated nod of approval, said, 'Well done.' I'd passed his test with flying colours. I think that was the game that made him realise I had something that a lot of young players don't have – awareness.

After that I thought I would drop back into the youth team, but Christmas came and went and I kept getting picked for the reserves. Slowly it dawned on me that my time watching the first team from the North Stand might soon be over. If that was going to be the case, I thought, then I should go out with a bang. At the next first-team game, I got myself nearer to the away fans than I'd ever been before.

As I've said, I wasn't a fighter, but I could feel a right hard nut with the fence between me and those travelling supporters. Getting a little carried away with my last hurrah, I started to get a bit brave and fired back the odd wanker sign in the away fans' direction. Eventually, my gesturing caught one particular bloke's eye and he started having a go back at me. It was then that I did something I'd seen Tony and the boys do. You know the one, a jab of the finger in their direction followed by a point down towards the bottom of the stand. I'm mouthing, 'Oi you! On the pitch now!' Then, to my absolute horror, he started to do the same back.

Trying to keep up the hard-man act, I started to walk down the steps of the North Stand, continuing the gesture. The problem was, he started walking down the steps mirroring my actions. *Oh no, he's actually going. Tone?* I looked around, but my brother was nowhere to be seen. *How am I going to blag this?* I couldn't go down there and fight, but I couldn't lose face either. Thinking on my feet, I slowed right down and pretended that someone else had pissed me off. I turned towards this fictional person in the crowd and started gesturing to them that I'd see them outside and quickly faded back into the sea of people.

For the rest of the game I was bricking it. *If that bloke recognises me outside I'm dead.* When the match finished, I went into the toilets, turned my coat inside out and wetted my hair down. Disguise complete, I thought through my plan. *Right, they go up Alderman Road and I go up Portman Road to go left. We could collide.* So instead I went all the way up St Matthew's Street, all the way up Norwich Road and came back down to my house. A journey that should have taken two minutes took me half an hour. That shows you how much of a fighter I was!

On 21 January, I scored both goals for the reserves in a 2-1 win against Birmingham. A week later, the first team were dumped out of the FA Cup, losing 2-0 at Second Division side Shrewsbury in the fourth round. That's when I got the call.

'You're having Thursday off school.' *All right.* 'You're going to train with the first team.' *OK.* It didn't seem real. I'd gone through the youth team and the reserves in the space of a few months. Now I was in with the big boys. I thought I'd done OK. I thought I'd survived. But I never saw that coming.

On that Thursday I walked down from my house on London Road to the ground, stomach full of butterflies, head spinning. I got into the building, made my way down the corridor towards the changing rooms then, at the last moment,

I turned right into the boiler room. There I hid in among the towels, paralysed with fear.

This is a little kid preparing to walk into the dressing room of one of the best teams in Europe that he'd grown up idolising. I stayed in that boiler room for about 25 minutes, semi-crouched behind the towel rack, thinking, 'Someone please come and get me.' In the end the kitman probably saw my afro poking over the top. 'Jason, is that you?' he called out. 'Yeah, I'm just looking for a towel,' I lied in response. 'Come on then, I'll take you in.'

Bobby Ferguson introduced me to the squad as I stood there awkwardly. They'd just been on the end of an embarrassing cup upset and were probably thinking, 'Who is this kid?' That's what was going through my mind, anyway. I got changed feeling sick. I knew I now had to try and get the better of Terry Butcher and Russell Osman. I'd watched these two at close quarters and knew they were hard as nails. Just like that reserves game at Chelsea, my thought process was, 'How can I not get kicked?' Again, that one-touch mentality got me through it.

Things had escalated real quick. Incredibly though, a whirlwind few months didn't end there.

7

The Goal That Changed Everything

AT THE end of that first training session with the first team, Bobby Ferguson announced his squad for Saturday's home game against Coventry City. It caught me by surprise when my name was among those read out. Again, I was in a bit of a daze. *Right, OK, this is happening now.*

Back then you only had one sub, but around 15 players would report on a matchday. There was absolutely no doubt in my mind, therefore, that this was Bobby just giving me a little taster as one of the three extra men.

With that in mind, I was relatively relaxed on the walk down to the ground. There was more excitement than nerves this time. I was just thinking, 'Let's see what this is all about.'

First up was the pre-match meal at 12 o'clock. That boiled chicken and beans was like caviar to me, honestly. It was way better than my usual fare of fish fingers and chips or a fry-up. *I'm living like a king here!* I tucked into that food quick. Halfway through rushing it down I glanced up and everyone – and I mean everyone – was staring at me like, 'Does he not get fed?' 'Slow down boy, come up from breath!' laughed Eric Gates.

After that, we all went into the players' lounge for an hour. Normally at that time on a Saturday I would be watching *Football Focus*. Naively, I assumed that's what would be on. But when I walked in, I saw Eric Gates and Paul Cooper looking at the TV going nuts, jumping up and down, excitedly punching the air and flicking their fingers. 'Come on number two!' They were watching the horses. Ah, no *Football Focus* for me then. I could hardly say 'can you turn the TV over?' could I?

An hour and a half before kick-off, Bobby Ferguson named the team. I was still pretty calm, just taking it all in and enjoying the experience.

'Cooper, Burley, Butcher, Osman, McCall.'

I nervously fiddled with the top of my socks, glancing up at each of my heroes as their names were read out, taking in how each of them was preparing and still not quite believing that I was there to witness all this.

'Wark, Putney, Brennan, O'Callaghan, Gates and Mariner.'

At this stage I was starting to think about the warm-up and whether I'd be able to spot my brother and mates in the crowd.

'And sub today is Dozzell.'

You what? It's like time stood still. I was not expecting that.

One of my first thoughts was that there were some established reserve players in that dressing room and I'd jumped the queue. This was a snub to them. The looks they gave me did not hide that fact.

Were they better than me? I don't know. I hadn't played with them enough to know. There were certainly a lot more experienced players Bobby could have turned to before me, though.

The warm-up was a bit of a blur. Then the teams lined up, I took my place on the bench wrapped up in a big jacket and eventually my emotions settled. *OK, I'm sub. This will be an experience.* I was sitting there nice and tall, full of pride, gazing at the North Stand, knowing all my mates and family were in there. *Maybe I'll get five minutes at the end? That would be great! No, you probably won't get on the pitch Jason, don't get carried away.* Those were the thoughts that were racing through my mind in the early stages of that game.

Paul Mariner put us 1-0 up in the 13th minute. Two minutes later, Mark Brennan doubled our advantage. By this point, I was just enjoying an entertaining game. Then, with 29 minutes gone, Eric Gates pulled up with a groin injury. It soon became apparent that he couldn't continue. Slowly it dawned on me. *I'm on.* I wasn't prepared at all. My socks were rolled down, my shin pads weren't on. I was scrambling about trying to get ready. I don't think I even did a single stretch. Suddenly, I was on the pitch.

OK, here we go.

To start with the order of the day, as always, was to play nice and early. *Nothing spectacular. Don't overcomplicate it. Get yourself in the game.* As I headed off at half-time, the score still 2-0, the first person I saw was Roy Knightsbridge. I think he'd muscled his way down to the tunnel entrance to make sure he could say a few words of encouragement. That was nice.

I don't remember much from Bobby's half-time team talk. I do remember Mariner, who had really hurt his ribs, having to go and play as a virtual passenger on the wing because we'd used our one sub.

Terry Gibson's chip got Coventry back to 2-1 in the 71st minute. As the game went on, my mindset switched. *Come on Jason, what have you got? Make a mark. Don't just have an average game. Don't just pop it off. Do something that is going to make everybody remember you. Do something monstrous.*

Eventually, the action reached the 89th minute. I'd done OK, but I wanted a little bit more. I wanted to score at that North Stand end. I knew if I did it would be massive. *Just give me one chance.*

We were awarded a deep free kick. Terry Butcher knocked a diagonal ball forwards, Johnny Wark won the header and suddenly the ball was bouncing. Me and the defender were in a race, shoulder-to-shoulder, to get there first. I slid in with my long legs, got a foot on it just ahead of him and hooked it over the keeper's head. For the second time that day, time stood still.

Then the ball landed in the net.

I can't remember what I did next. It was a complete blur. Just pure emotion. I don't think I did a lot as a celebration. I just looked up at the North Stand.

I was mobbed as I left the field. There were plenty more back slaps and congratulations when I made it to the dressing room too. Bobby Ferguson knew the media would all be waiting for me outside, so he turned to Russell Osman and said, 'Get him home.'

Russell's wife worked for Mercedes and he always had the best cars. I followed him out the back door, climbed in the front of this big Jeep-type thing and he told me, 'No, Bobby says hide in the back.' So I did as I was told, got in the back and crouched down in the footwell. Three days earlier I'd been hiding from Russell in the boiler room. Now he's the one helping me do the hiding! It was all so surreal.

Russell dropped me at my house. Mum and Tootie were waiting outside to greet me and probably wondered what on earth was going on when I unfolded myself and clambered out the back door. It still hadn't really sunk in what had just happened. Kirpal Singh was a friend of mine and his parents had a little shop just around the corner with a pool table down in the cellar. So me and Pasquale went over to see him and, just as three normal 16-year-old boys would do, we played pool on a Saturday night. It was like nothing had happened.

I slept, got up and grabbed my boots to go and play for Langham Lions. It was 'Super Sunday' after all. I wanted to play for Roy because he'd set me off on this journey. But when I got to the ground there were journalists there. I decided not to play because I didn't think Ipswich would be happy.

On the way home I went and got all the papers. Obviously, I turned straight to the sport. It was such a buzz seeing 'Roy of the Rovers' headlines and 'Dozzell 89' in the results sections. Eventually, I started flicking through the news pages and, just as I was about to stop, something in the *News of the World* caught my eye. There was a double-page spread. 'He lives on mince and milkshakes' was the headline. They'd got hold of my mum. No doubt she probably got a few quid for that.

As I read those papers, I imagined the opposition fan I'd confronted in the North Stand just a few weeks earlier seeing my picture and thinking, 'That's the cheeky little sod who offered me on the pitch.' I'm sure there were a fair few Ipswich fans also thinking, 'Isn't he the kid who normally stands near us?' It made me smile. I also wondered when I'd next be back in that North Stand with them.

I was back at Chantry High School on the Monday. Mum told me I'd better look smart, so for the first time ever I wore shoes, a nice pair of trousers and a nice jacket. That wasn't me. I never dressed up.

When I got in, I was told 'the TV cameras are here'. At playtime they got the whole school out, every single pupil, to make a circle for me. The TV people wanted me to do some keepy-uppies in the middle. Could I manage that in those shoes? Not a chance. There was this flap-over bit at the front of them with a big button and the ball was going everywhere. They were probably all thinking, 'This kid just scored in a First Division game, really?'

It was embarrassing. I ended up taking the shoes off and playing in socks. Then I got my keep-ups going. A few kicks, a few knees, a few headers. That was that. I was badly out of my comfort zone, but was thinking, 'Come on, you've just played at Portman Road, you can do this.'

The way everyone was with me changed that day. Teachers, the popular kids, girls – now everybody wanted to know me and be nice.

A shy, quiet, reserved, socially awkward kid had been thrust into the limelight. Adoration had started. Money would follow.

That was the goal that changed everything.

8

Bobby's Golden Child

I DID an interview on Radio Orwell a few days after my debut goal. That was scarier than playing. I could barely string two words together. Bobby Ferguson rang up Tony Dable at the school afterwards and apparently said something along the lines of, 'What the hell are you doing letting him go on the radio?' (but in slightly more colourful terms). Tony gently reminded Bobby that I might have been at Luton were it not for him. Fair point. That was an early sign of Bobby's protective instincts towards me, though.

A few weeks later the club had pulled me out of school. There was no one in my life, personally or professionally, saying it might be a good idea to get some qualifications. That would never happen with a young footballer today.

I regret it now, but back then I obviously thought it was great. No exams! All I was thinking was, 'I get to play with these players every day now, I will get better.' It took me a while to get up to their rhythm though. Nothing can prepare you for that step up. There's so much more pace on the passes. *Whack!* And you're expected to deal with it every time.

I told them they were my heroes. I still do today. You can't fake it when you're in awe of someone. They know. I maybe got a bit of respect back because they were the same sort of age as my brother and, chances are, would have known of his reputation. People talk. Tony would come to the players' lounge after games, so I think they soon put two and two together.

It wasn't long until I was heading to Chelmsford in a car with experienced duo Paul Cooper and Eric Gates, plus a young Mark Brennan for a drinking session. Me having not long turned 16 didn't stop an invite coming my way.

I could already see how dressing rooms worked. No matter how old you were, managers wanted players who had a bit about them. I was reserved, quiet. I could see that I wasn't going to fit in and I'm 100 per cent a person who goes with the crowd to fit in. I didn't want them to think I was just a kid. I knew I had to act differently, so I started having a few beers with my team-mates now and again for a bit of Dutch courage.

In those days you could get eaten alive. You've got 30 guys and the banter could be quite brutal. It could get quite personal too. There could be comments about your mum, or this or that. If you're not strong-willed it can be quite hard. The bigger characters in the group will challenge you.

Trevor Putney was the main man. From the minute you got in for training to the moment you left, he just did not stop. He was so hyperactive. He used to do this thing where he'd put his head on the treatment table and his legs on the roof, twist them round and do a Fergie impersonation. You had to be there I guess, but trust me, it was hilarious.

Putters was the one who gave me my nickname – 'Mr Magoo'. My eyes went quite early, but I didn't get them tested so I used to walk around squinting just like the fictional cartoon character. It was so bad that on the pitch I was running into people. I got away with it for a year or so somehow until the club made me see someone. Then the first time I put contact lenses in it was like, 'Jesus, is that what things are supposed to look like?!'

A bit of banter aside, the first-team players were great with me. I could sense some resentment from the reserve-team lads, though. That was only natural given this skinny little kid had overtaken them. If you're a 20-year-old trying to get in the first team and a 16-year-old leaps over you then you're going to be thinking, 'OK, maybe my time is done here.'

Up to 17, I had to stay on a £25-a-week youth contract. But I could get the first team bonuses – £100 an appearance, £200 a win – on top of that. All us youth-teamers would go and collect our money in cash from the office at the end of each month. Everyone else would be getting their £100, while some months I'd have this fat envelope stacked with as much £1,500. That was always awkward.

After my debut, I dipped in and out of the first-team squad for the next few matches. I came on in defeats against Stoke, West Ham, Luton and Everton – all away – then Bobby put me back in the reserves and youth squads for a breather. I think, much like with that phone call to the school, he was trying to protect me after all the initial hype.

It didn't help that my first game for the club had been Paul Mariner's last in an Ipswich shirt. His move to Arsenal had been the worst-kept secret. There was a goodbye piece in the programme that night which turned out to be slightly premature. It wasn't long before the deal was completed, though. The *News of the World* report following my debut goal stated, 'If Mariner really is on his way, Ipswich already have a ready-made replacement in schoolboy Jason Dozzell.'

I wasn't too happy about that comparison. That could be interpreted as 'he's ready to step in'. People maybe got the wrong idea, thinking the club had sold Paul so they could get me in. I couldn't fill his boots. This was an Ipswich legend and an established England international who'd just been to the last World Cup. I was nowhere near ready physically.

We finished that season in 12th. It was only the second time in 12 years that Ipswich had finished in the bottom half. A cycle was coming to an end. With the newly developed Pioneer Stand needing to be paid off, the great team of the late '70s and early '80s rapidly began to break up.

Mick Mills and Arnold Mühren had gone to Southampton and Manchester United respectively in 1982, while Frans Thijssen and Alan Brazil left for Forest and Tottenham the following year. A month after Mariner had gone to Arsenal, Johnny Wark signed for Liverpool. I was absolutely gutted about those two going, but on the flip side I also knew it could open the door for me and some of the other young lads coming through.

At the start of the 1984/85 season, I went with the first team full-time and it wasn't long before I was being dubbed Bobby's 'golden child'. While the other youth-teamers were made to clean boots and sweep up the dressing rooms, I was assigned the plum task of tidying up Bobby's office. All I had to do was go in there and pick up a few bits and even that 'job' went altogether after a while. Again, you can imagine how that went down with the other players my age. The first team would leave all this mess for them to clear up after training and I just went straight home.

Bobby was tough. He didn't mince his words when he wasn't happy. I saw other players get killed by him. Frank Yallop and Irvin Gernin – Jesus Christ! – I don't know if it was a full-back thing, but he used to tear into them badly. Putney was another who got pelters because he was a bit of a livewire and I'm not too sure if Bobby liked Cockneys. He was always calling him a Cockney this and a Cockney that.

One time, I played in a reserves game and Putters got up to where the mic was for the PA system. Mark Grew made a save and Putters' voice came out through the speakers. 'Great save, Barney.' Fergie went nuts. 'Putttnney!' he roared, sprinting up the stairs. He absolutely destroyed him for that. Those two had a real love–hate relationship.

By contrast, I was undoubtedly one of Bobby's favourites. He actually gave me chocolates on my birthday once. It was really embarrassing at times. He'd be doing the post-match analysis on a Monday and there'd be a clip where we're defending a free kick. I'm literally just standing in the wall, the same as the others. Bobby would pause it and, all animated, say to the rest of the lads, 'Just look at the way he's standing so tall! Look! That's what we want!' I wanted the ground to open and swallow me up. I could see everyone looking at each other, smirking. They would take the piss a bit afterwards.

'Well played golden boy,' and, 'How's your dad?' What could I say? I just tried to laugh it off.

Bobby, just like Roy Knightsbridge and Tony Dable, recognised that I was a vulnerable kid who needed to be shown a bit of love. And I loved him for that. He was another father figure to me, which is exactly what I needed at that time.

On 9 December 1984 – my 17th birthday – I signed my first professional contract. There's a nice picture of Bobby standing there with a proud arm on my shoulder with Charlie Woods also looking on. Bobby's quote in the papers the next day was, 'Jason has got the potential to become a very good First Division footballer. He is potentially one of the best players we have had at the club and now he's got to go out and prove himself.' No pressure then! Having dipped me out of the first team for a spell, he obviously thought I was ready to go again.

Six days later, Alan Sunderland, who had come in on loan from Arsenal to fill the Mariner void up front, limped off in a 2-0 home defeat to Sunderland. The *Green 'Un* report of that game states, 'The biggest cheer of the afternoon was when Dozzell came on.'

It was time for my full debut. Who were we playing next? Manchester United away. Wow! I'm up against Bryan Robson, one of my England idols growing up, as well as the likes of Frank Stapleton and Gordon McQueen. Arnold Mühren, one of my Ipswich heroes, was on the bench for them. There was a crowd of 35,000 at Old Trafford. Talk about a baptism of fire. Mind you, George Burley's debut for Ipswich was also as a 17-year-old at Manchester United and he was up against George Best, so he had it tougher than me!

What an experience that was. We hit the post twice and had one cleared off the line, all at 0-0, before eventually getting beat 3-0 following some late goals. It was one of those defeats that you come away from with plenty of praise. I felt I'd given a good account of myself.

My main memory from that day is from half-time. Bobby came striding into the changing room with his head down and, as usual, started hammering people. The problem was that he was in the wrong changing room. He was talking to Manchester United's Remi Moses, thinking it was Romeo Zondervan! Eventually the penny dropped. 'Sorry boys!' He came marching over to see us and we were all trying to keep straight faces. That was typical Bobby.

After that came my first Christmas party. Now that was an education. We met early doors at the Chequers pub on the road heading out to Needham Market; the drinking started early and went on all day. That was as big a baptism of fire as my full debut. I'd never really drunk like that before. I'd had the odd one here or there, but it hadn't really been for me. Eventually we all went for an Indian meal. Again, it was a new culinary experience. I just about kept the food down and thankfully that helped sober me up.

I started the next two festive fixtures – a 2-0 loss at Forest on Boxing Day followed by another defeat by the same scoreline at home to Everton – and, all of a sudden, a massive New Year's Day game was staring me in the face. The East Anglian derby at Portman Road.

Norwich meant a bit more to me because of my history. It was deep-rooted for me, very deep-rooted. I knew this rivalry was more than just intense. It was hate. I'd seen it first-hand. They're the enemy. Now I'm representing my hometown club in this fixture and my brother's on my case.

Gatesy put us 1-0 up very early on and flicked a V sign in the direction of the directors' box. I think he'd fallen out with the club about something. Then, midway through the second half, Romeo Zondervan headed the ball down and I swivelled to shoot and score. That was an incredible feeling. Better than my debut goal? Maybe. As a kid growing up I didn't dream of getting the record of being the youngest top-flight goalscorer. No, I'd dreamed of scoring against Norwich.

I was definitely a different person in every Norwich game I played. I was a lot more intense. I remember their manager at the time, Ken Brown, heaping praise on me after that match.

Four days later, I scored again with a crisp left-footed strike to secure a 2-1 win at Bristol Rovers in the FA Cup. That game was on a bad pitch and there was some trouble in the stands. Mark Brennan scored the winner from 35 yards out and there was some debate about whether he meant it. Looking back, that was Kevin Wilson's debut after we'd signed him from Derby.

The following week, I started in a home game against QPR in the quarter-final of the Milk Cup. It finished 0-0, but I'll always remember it because that was the first (and not last) time that Tony ended up on the pitch. Chelsea's game had been cancelled that day and apparently their hooligans decided to come to ours for a fight with QPR instead. It all kicked off in the stands and, on this occasion, it ended up spilling on to the field of play. Just as I was shaping to receive a throw-in,

I heard this commotion, looked around and saw a bunch of fans scrapping just yards away. Immediately, I saw my brother's ginger hair in among the melee. Of course he was involved. I didn't know what to do. Do I look at what's going on over there or do I trap the ball? Thankfully, the game soon got stopped. This was my sixth start in senior football!

I scored again in the next round of the FA Cup later that month as we beat Gillingham 3-2 at home to reach the fifth round. The Third Division visitors had come from 2-0 down to level things up before my swerving winner, which came following a Mich d'Avray knock-down. 'It was just reward for Dozzell, who had looked elegant and assured in midfield,' wrote Philip Osborn in the *Sunday Express* under a headline that read, 'Teenage Jason Toast of Town'. The verdict from Julie Welch, in *The Observer*, was more a case of damning with faint praise, 'The difference between the two sides was ultimately Dozzell, who is still a bit gangly and uncoordinated around five-sixths of the pitch, but once he gets near goal is as deadly as a heat-seeking missile.'

I don't know what it was about the FA Cup, but it was a competition I got a lot of joy from over the years. I ended up scoring 13 goals in it altogether. It must have been the inspiration of '78, I think. I loved knockout football.

By the time February rolled around the team was in good form and I was starting to feel like I belonged. Now we were preparing to take on Norwich in a two-legged Milk Cup semi-final.

Bragging rights and a place at Wembley were at stake. This was huge.

We beat them 1-0 at Portman Road courtesy of Mich d'Avray's early goal. It was my tenth successive start. Then I was dropped for the next two games – quickfire home wins against Chelsea and Sheffield Wednesday, the latter putting us in the quarter-finals of the FA Cup. Squad morale was high ahead of the return trip to Carrow Road. I wasn't sure whether I'd be picked, though.

Around 13,000 Ipswich fans went up to Norfolk for that game, most of them just hanging around the ground. I was delighted when Bobby said I was back in the team. I won't lie though, as he was giving his team talk, I was worrying about what my brother was up to outside.

During games I was always thinking, 'Is he going to be OK?' I'd know where he was sitting and be glancing up during breaks in the play. Because I'd sorted the tickets for him and his mates, my concern would be, 'If they get in trouble, am I going to get in trouble?' Now I was playing, he faced even more provocation. Opposition fans would always try and wind him up and say, 'Your brother's shit.' He had to try and learn to be cool. Sadly, that often proved difficult for Tony. I'll talk more about that later.

In that second leg against Norwich, I got bullied by Asa Hartford, proper bullied. He was an old-school player. They tried to kick us off the park and at times it went over the top. John Deehan made it 1-1 on aggregate then, in the 87th minute, they got a corner. I got blocked off, Steve Bruce ran off me and headed in their winner.

For some reason we were put in portacabins that day. There must have been building work at their stadium or something.

Terry Butcher went ballistic. That's the angriest I've ever seen him. He kicked the door off its hinges and punched a hole in the wall. Outside it was all kicking off too. I don't think there were any shop windows left in Norwich city centre come the next morning.

To this day I don't know why it was me, a kid just out of school, who was assigned to mark Steve Bruce. Yes, I could compete in the air, but marking one of the best headers of the ball in football at that time was a different story. I was in bits. I blamed myself for the fact we weren't going to Wembley. To make matters worse, we'd lost to *them*. If I could go back and replay any game in my career it would definitely be that one.

It had been one high after another up until then for me, but that was my first big lesson about the lows of the game. This is football, kid.

There was no time to feel sorry for ourselves, though. We went straight into an FA Cup quarter-final at Everton. I was dropped. That finished 2-2. I didn't start the replay either. We lost 1-0 and, with all knockout dreams ended, the reality of a relegation fight hit home.

When you've had a proper taste of senior football and then get taken out the team that's hard to take, but Bobby explained to me that I wasn't going to play every game because I was still very young and assured me that I was miles ahead of schedule. I accepted that.

I returned to the starting line-up at Arsenal for a Tuesday night game in mid-March. Seeing the famous marble halls at Highbury was another big 'wow' moment. Paul Mariner played for them. We went 1-0 down, but I managed to get the equaliser with a decent finish. Reading the *East Anglian Daily Times* match report back reminds me of how good the move was. Dave Allard wrote, 'Burley broke from the right-back position to hold off a challenge from former team-mate Mariner and then sprayed the ball out to Dozzell, who had taken up a position a third of the way into the Arsenal half out towards the left. Under instructions from experienced team-mate Gates, Dozzell was told to hold on to the ball, while Gates himself made a run. Just at the right time, the youngster released the ball to his little team-mate and Gates burst past Tony Adams to whip over a cross from near the byline which Dozzell, who had followed up cunningly, swept into the net past the hapless John Lukic. It was a peach of a goal guaranteed to water the mouths of football fans anywhere.' He added, 'Dozzell showed some marvellous touches, the highlight being when he killed a low, driven cross from Zondervan and turned the ball into Gates's path in a split second.'

That report also jogged my memory of the Arsenal fans chanting 'what a load of rubbish' at the half-time whistle and calling for Brian Talbot to come on. Brian, of course, was another of the Ipswich players I'd watched in the '78 FA Cup Final. Having started off playing alongside my heroes, I now seemed to be facing quite a few of them.

I didn't play a lot more for the first team that season. I wasn't in the squad when we got a little bit of revenge on Norwich in the league. I did, however, get off the bench in a 3-2 win at Tottenham where I got to face the likes of Glenn Hoddle and World Cup winner Ossie Ardiles. Hoddle left me dizzy. I was drooling at some of the stuff he was doing.

I was quite good at that silky part of the game, but he was exceptional at it. That made me realise how far I had to go.

I was put back in the youth team for big games and I loved it. We had Craig Forrest in goal, while in attack it was me, Dalian Atkinson and Michael Cole – three black lads. Just like Cyrille Regis, Laurie Cunningham and Brendon Batson at West Brom in the '70s, we were dubbed 'The Three Degrees' by the press. That was the headline in every paper. 'The Three Degrees strike again'. Not something that's aged well, but that's just how it was then. It didn't bother me.

That team tore it up. We got to a South East Counties Cup Final and faced Tottenham at Kenilworth Road. Spurs had the best youth teams in those days and a lot of that side went on to have senior careers, but we annihilated them to claim the trophy. The scoreline of 3-2 really doesn't do justice to how well we played.

After that, we got a late call to play in a competition in France because another team had dropped out, so we flew straight there from Luton. Barcelona, Porto, Rangers – all the big guns were involved. How we got a 0-0 against Barcelona I will never know. We were hanging on for our lives. Then we beat Porto 2-0 in the final. That was amazing. Michael Cole was named player of the tournament. We felt the bee's knees.

The first team, meanwhile, finished 17th, just a point above the relegation zone. Russell Osman and Eric Gates duly signed for Leicester and Sunderland respectively that summer. All eyes were now firmly on the next crop of youngsters coming through.

9

The Man With the Scar

THE COUNTY of Suffolk, with its population of more than 750,000, has just one professional football club – Ipswich Town.

Travel 14 miles east of Ipswich and you hit Felixstowe, home of the UK's largest container port, and, beyond, the North Sea. Go west, along the A14, and it's 55 miles before you reach Cambridge. That's a city known globally for its university, not its football. Head south, down the A12, and it's 16 miles before you cross the border into Essex and find Colchester, a town famed for its Roman roots and army barracks. Journey north, into Norfolk, and it's 45 miles before the cathedral city of Norwich is found.

Think of Ipswich though and you think of Ipswich Town Football Club. Portman Road, fittingly, is the first thing you see when you walk out of the train station. The club is literally at the heart of the community. It's what's put the town on the map. So when you play for Ipswich Town, it's impossible to walk around without being noticed. Even more so when you're a local boy.

Most people stop and talk, politely passing on their well wishes. Others are slightly more awkward. These days, players probably get a picture or video taken of them on the sly that soon gets posted on social media. Back in my day, without camera phones, it was just a double take, followed by some pointing and gesturing that was far less subtle than they probably imagined.

My first experience of that came after I'd scored on my debut aged 16. I was a shy, socially awkward, insecure kid suddenly getting all this attention. *What's the fuss all about?* Eventually I realised that a smile and nod would make someone's day.

There was this one particular guy, however, whose lingering stare contained no warmth. He stuck in my mind because he had a prominent scar down one cheek. Every time we crossed paths he'd look at me real funny. *What's his problem?* I didn't have a clue who he was, but it turns out he knew all about me long before I'd become a footballer.

* * *

As a teenager, when I started coming up against some of the more streetwise lads in the teams from Essex and east London, I'd regularly get told, 'You don't know what colour you are.' It was the same at school. Two doors down from me was the Crossfield family; Rupert was my age, and we were the only black kids in our year. The older kids would make comments. Again, the one I often got was, 'You don't know what colour you are.'

They were right. I had darker skin than everyone else, but my mum's white – and I'm not going against her. I was confused. I didn't know anything about race. I didn't really give it a second thought.

When I went to watch Ipswich as a kid I'd see all these England flags in the away end that had 'NF' on them – 'Chelsea NF' and 'West Ham NF'. *That's weird.* To me, 'NF' meant Nottingham Forest. Why would another club put that on their flag? I had no idea what the National Front was. Start a conversation with me about the right wing and I'd be excitedly talking to you about West Brom's Laurie Cunningham getting paint on his boots.

Here's another example of how naive I was. All the 'skinheads' – many of whom started associating themselves with the National Front – used to wear slim-fit shirts, braces and Airwair Dr. Martens boots. I didn't understand what that represented, I thought it was just fashion, so I bought a pair myself!

This may sound a strange thing to say given what I've just outlined, but I didn't ask who my father was growing up. It wasn't even like I gently raised the topic and mum shut it down. It was just never broached. I was a sheltered kid with my head in the clouds. I didn't know anything about the world and it simply didn't occur to me to ask questions.

It was my sister, Tootie, who reached out to Dad first. I don't know how she tracked him down, but she did and it turned out he was in San Diego, California. That was in 1989 when I was 21 years old. He invited us over, but I didn't want to go. Maybe it was to protect my mum, maybe I didn't want to be disappointed. Whatever it was, I stayed at home.

Tootie went over though, came back with glowing reports and said, 'Just go, you'll regret it if you don't.' So, once the football season had finished, I flew out to the US to see him. That's when I discovered my roots and who the man with the scar was.

* * *

RAF Bentwaters was constructed in a remote part of the Suffolk countryside in 1942. The area was ideal for wartime flying operations given its flat East Anglian soil, sparse population and location just a few miles from the coast. After the Second World War, control of the base was handed over to the United States Air Force and it played a key role in the defence of western Europe during the Cold War.

Why am I telling you this? Because it was around 1962 – the year of the Cuban Missile Crisis – that my father, a maintenance worker for the military, was posted there.

Charles Dozzell was raised in Amarillo, Texas. *Where's that?* I had to look it up when he told me. I'd only heard of it because of that Tony Christie song. A quick look at the map showed me it was at the heart of the Texas Panhandle (the square bit at the top of the state that is bordered by New Mexico and Oklahoma).

Dad grew up in the US's Deep South at a time when racial segregation was still in force. As a young man, he had to adhere to signs that indicated where black people could legally walk, talk, rest and eat.

It was in 1955 that civil rights activist Rosa Parks refused to give up her seat on a public bus to a white passenger. Eight years later came Martin Luther King's 'I Have a Dream' speech. In between those two huge events, Dad crossed the Atlantic. He was a frustrated young man looking for a new beginning.

He knew nothing about England. Would there be black people there? Were they also treated like second-class citizens? He soon got his answer.

Dad didn't venture out of the barracks for months until eventually he plucked up the courage to make a day trip to London. He sent a letter back to his mum. 'Bloody hell, there's black people here!' Encouraged by that, he started making regular trips to Ipswich. It soon became clear, however, that a black American was not welcome. White people and the police, he says, were the least hospitable. Even the Jamaicans, who eventually became his mates, were against him to start with.

Allies, surprisingly, came in the form of an Irishman and a Scotsman. It sounds like the start of a bad joke, doesn't it? They were outcasts too though, so those three stuck together and looked after each other.

Dad found his feet. He met Mum. They fell in love. In the space of two years along came me and Tootie. We were all living happily on Woodbridge Road. Mum, following her previous troubles, was finally happy and settled.

Then came the incident that changed everything.

One night, Mum and Dad came out of the Manor Ballroom Picture House and started walking home hand-in-hand. It had been a lovely evening, but it soon turned sour as some white men took offence at this interracial couple's public show of affection. Obscenities were shouted. They were chased up the road. 'Get inside!' Dad shouted at Mum as they reached the house. But those men wouldn't leave it there. They threw sticks at the windows, one tried to get into the house, and there was an altercation. The other guy came off second best.

That was the man with the scar.

Someone trying to come into your house, with your partner and two young children inside. Personally, I call that self-defence. That's not how the police saw it, though. Dad ended up in jail. He was in there for about a year.

Is it possible to remember things from when you're two or three? I swear I can remember sitting in a pram visiting that prison. Maybe that's me inventing that image in my head once I heard the back story. I don't know.

When Dad got out of jail, he and Mum got married. They tied the knot, of all places, at Norwich registry office. But it was no use; the racial tensions remained and he continued to feel a target of hate. And so the decision was taken for him to go back to the US.

That's why it was just the three of us growing up.

* * *

Meeting Dad for the first time got off to a funny start.

When I got to the airport there was no one there. Had he changed his mind? I had to look through the American phone book for the name Dozzell. Eventually I got through to his house on a pay phone and discovered he was just running a bit late. It had been almost 20 years, what does a few more minutes matter, right?!

When he arrived it was emotional. A big hug. Lots of tears. When we got to his place he told me the story I just told you.

I didn't ask if he'd tried to contact us when we were growing up. I think he did because of how delighted he was to hear from us, the way he welcomed me into the family and the pride I saw in him as my football career progressed. I didn't ask Mum because I knew what answer I'd get from her. I think she was just trying to protect us.

As soon as I walked out of that airport the intense heat hit me. There were palm trees lining the street and it just looked so lush. Then I saw the beaches. Wow. I immediately fell in love with America.

I had two weeks over there meeting this big family I never knew about. There were aunties, grandparents, great-grandparents. I seemed to be introduced to someone new every day. I'd gone all through my life thinking I hadn't got any family at all to suddenly being on the other side of the world playing golf with my granddad and eating my nan's homemade tacos. It was pretty overwhelming, but also great.

It turned out my dad was an American football coach and my younger brother Marcus was a very gifted player. Marcus and I got on great and he really helped put me at ease. When I got home, I sent him £1,000 as a goodwill gesture. Later on, God, did I get that back tenfold. Marcus went on to do really well for himself – some water business or something, I'm not entirely sure. Again, I don't ask questions. Whenever I went over to visit he'd pick me up in a white Bentley and we'd drive to Vegas. It quickly became clear to me that he was someone who didn't have to queue for anything. It was pool parties by day and casinos at night. We had the best time.

I've got a personality that means I am drawn to excitement. I like fun. I soon saw where I got that gene from. It became apparent that my dad likes a good time too. He'd come out with Marcus and me to the nightclubs. We'd talk about our life experiences, but it never got too deep. Generally, we just partied.

Sometimes it's a toss of a coin if these sort of reunions work out. You do hear horror stories about people meeting their dad for the first time later in life and not getting on, but this scenario played out well.

I absolutely loved those two weeks in San Diego. The beaches, the barbecues – it was magical. I went back home for the start of pre-season training ahead of the 1988/89 campaign thinking, 'I can't wait for this season to finish so I can go over again.'

I returned from that trip not only feeling different, but looking different, too. Big baggy jeans down below my bum, basketball and NFL tops paired with baseball caps – my mates must have thought I looked like a right Yank!

I went over every year religiously after that. Dad finally came over here in 1993 for my wedding. He had to get clearance from the authorities because of his previous conviction. He was here for three weeks and, again, it was just magical.

It wasn't all great when I went over there, though. Further down the line, at a time when I'd split from my wife in the 2000s, I went over to the US to clear my head, but it turned out Dad was also having trouble with his wife. We went to

Vegas to see Marcus, had a brilliant time, got back to San Diego and the house had been stripped bare. All the furniture. Everything. Gone. She'd left him and he was nearly crying. I was shocked. We both looked at each other as if to say, 'What is going on?' That was a sad trip.

I carried on going out there every year, but after my wedding he'd come to visit me every fourth or fifth year. He loved England and reconnected with some old friends from his time here originally. It was great to hear them reminisce about back in the day, telling brilliant stories with so much laughter.

* * *

Once my football career finished, and I started to accumulate a bit of mental baggage, my visits to the US started to become more sporadic. It's when I had time to reflect, when I didn't start to feel good, that slowly I began to isolate. I wanted to stay away from things that were deep.

Come 2017 it had been six years since I'd last seen Dad. An opportunity arose for us to reconnect, but this reunion got off to an even bigger false start than the first.

I'd been invited on an incredible trip by a guy called Gary Harvey. Gary was the AFC Sudbury manager when they got to all those FA Vase finals back in the mid-2000s, had a box at Ipswich Town and used to invite me to that now and again. We became friends.

Gary owns an engineering company and is not short of a few quid. One day he decided to pay for 15 guys to go to Vegas, no expense spared. We stayed at Caesar's Palace, went to Gordon Ramsay's restaurant and had the red rope VIP treatment with thousands of pounds put behind the bar. As I said, Marcus was a well-respected figure around town and it wouldn't be long before he was giving security a little nod to let a few girls join us in our booth.

It was at the first pool party of that trip that I'd arranged for Dad to come and meet me, but things didn't go according to plan. The drinks were flowing, I was having some banter with this group of Manchester United fans and it ended up with me getting pushed in the pool with my phone in my pocket. 'That's broken then,' I thought. 'Ah well. Get me another drink.'

Soon I was dying for a slash, but the toilets were rammed. Stupidly, I tried to duck around the corner and do one where I shouldn't have done. It's the US, isn't it? They don't mess about with that. The same security guys who, just a minute earlier, had been bringing women over to our table, now had my hands behind my back and were manhandling me towards the exit. *That escalated quickly.*

Here's the best part. Just at the exact moment I was getting frogmarched out, my dad was walking in. He was with my eldest son Dion too, who was over on a soccer scholarship in America at the time and had flown across from Florida. Remember, this is the first time I'd seen Dad in six years. 'All right!' was all I could get out, with a sheepish drunken grin, as we crossed paths. I was absolutely trollied.

Thankfully they didn't take me to the station, but I'd been kicked out of this party. Marcus came out and drove me back to the hotel. I had a sleep and sobered up, but when I woke up I realised I had no phone to get in contact with anyone.

Just like almost 30 years earlier, I found myself using a pay phone to rectify the situation. This time it was a call home, a quick explanation of what had happened, followed by one of my other sons contacting one of the members of our group on Instagram. Eventually, someone came and got me.

Did connecting with my dad at 21 fill a hole in my life? Definitely. Don't get me wrong though, it didn't fix everything. I think about all the little things I missed growing up. You always wonder 'what if?' What if I'd had this extended family unit and father figure guiding me?

Later in life, when I reached my dark place, I probably should have reached out to him more. He probably has no idea how bad things got for me. As I said, I started to pull away from everyone and isolated myself. With Dad I always told myself, 'He's 5,000 miles away, he can't help.' That's on me.

He was last over here in September 2022. That visit didn't start particularly well. I had stuff going on in my life, my girlfriend was going through a messy divorce, and seeing your dad who you don't see that often is quite heavy.

There were times when we clashed a little bit, I can't lie, and that was probably because of me. I'm used to living on my own. I was going to work, coming home and didn't have the space I'm used to. By contrast, he'd been stuck inside all day. It just made for the perfect storm.

We had a petty argument – my fault, 100 per cent I started it – and were both standing our ground. Then something amazing happened. He got up off his seat, strode over and, with me half expecting him to square up, he gave me the biggest hug in the world. *Wow*. A weird feeling went through me. 'That felt good,' I thought. *Actually, that felt great.* Something lifted from me with that hug. Something changed.

I didn't know it, but that was something I'd probably been dying for. Because after that I felt, 'This is it, I've got a dad.' That's all I needed. That one big hug seemed to change my perception of our relationship. I'd been waiting for that interaction. For years we'd just had a good time, but I needed something more.

When my dad hugged me, what a difference that made. I was pretty old before I realised how I could make people feel with hugs and affection. I used to go out on Saturdays and see a family having a meal and think 'that looks boring'. I just wanted to have fun, but I had it the wrong way around. You have to involve family. You have to do things collectively. Not every week, but it's important.

I'm not the only one in the family who hasn't had stable relationships throughout their life. A lot of my brothers and sisters are the same. We've all tried, but there's not been longevity. I think we're a bit dysfunctional because we weren't shown what's normal.

I'm definitely a visual kind of guy. It's not what you say to me, it's what you show me. I think it's important as a kid growing up to see things – like a mum and dad holding hands – to understand how relationships work for when you get older. You've got the tools then.

Sometimes I could be scared of affection because I wasn't used to it. 'Scared' is probably the wrong word, actually. 'Uncomfortable' is better. I think that's what we've all been like. We don't know how to handle it when someone holds our hands.

Nowadays I'm all over it when it comes to showing affection to my kids and my girlfriend. It took me a while to understand that's the way it's got to be. Respecting women, this is how it's got to be done. It took a lot of trial and error for me to reach that point.

If that hug with my dad hadn't happened I reckon our relationship might have drifted. We'd still have stayed in touch, but there would probably have been fewer and fewer phone calls and trips.

It's funny, isn't it? I wasn't prepared for that visit. It felt like he was coming over at the worst possible time. But I'm glad it happened now because out of it I got something huge. That moment seemed to ignite me again. I felt it and I think he felt it too.

Dressed up for the FA Cup Final in 1978. You can see why someone in the row behind wanted me to take that hat off! Personal

Celebrating cup success with Ranelagh Road Primary School in 1979. A time when everything I touched seemed to turn to gold. Newsquest

Fresh from a trip to Adam and Eves to get my hair blow dried. I probably got the Jheri curl out as soon as this photoshoot was over.
Personal

More pictures from my mum's scrapbook, including meeting Ipswich Town captain Mick Mills with other members of the Junior Blues. Mick's a legend and one of my heroes, but some of his comments about Andre on the radio disappointed me a few years ago.
Personal

Meeting my new Langham Lions team-mates for the first time in 1980. The size difference seems funny now, but it didn't then. Contributed by Roy Knightsbridge

Being sent on for my debut, aged 16 and 57 days, by Bobby Ferguson in February 1984. It wasn't until years later that I realised the magnitude of what he'd done.
Newsquest

Pictured not long after being thrust into the action. All subs wore the number 12 in those days – there was only one!
Newsquest

With my Langham Lions manager Roy Knightsbridge at half-time of my debut. Roy was a father figure to me as a kid.
Contributed by Roy Knightsbridge

My debut goal looping into the net. It was one of those moments where time seemed to stand still.
Newsquest

Springing to my feet in celebration. I knew I'd done something monstrous.
Newsquest

Mobbed as I left the field. It wasn't long before I was hiding in the back of Russell Osman's car.
Newsquest

Back at Chantry High School on the Monday. Doing keep-ups in front of the TV cameras was a challenge!

Scrubbing boots as a 16-year-old in 1984. It wasn't long before I escaped such duties and was assigned the plum task of tidying Bobby Ferguson's office.
Newsquest

Signing my first professional contract on my 17th birthday, flanked by a proud-looking Bobby Ferguson and Charlie Woods.
Newsquest

How the East Anglian Daily Times *reported on me scoring against Norwich City at the age of 17.* East Anglian Daily Times

Page 30 East Anglian Daily Times, Wednesday, January 2, 1985

Ipswich lift gloom with glorious win

Ipswich 2 Norwich 0

BATTLING Ipswich Town celebrated the New Year with a heartwarming home win over Norwich City in a muddy, blood and thunder local derby at Portman Road yesterday.

Bobby Ferguson's side hauled themselves out of the bottom three of the table on goal difference and the 21,710 crowd were shown plenty of reasons why 1985 just might not be such a gloomy prospect as some pundits would have us believe.

By Dave Allard

What a difference an early goal makes, and Eric Gates' third minute effort ended a home run without a league goal that stretches back to the 3-3 home draw with Watford on November 3 . . . the gloomy total of six hours and 18 minutes of home football to be precise.

That early breakthrough was just the spark the team needed to launch them into 90 minutes of undying effort and in the 65th minute Jason Dozzell, the blossoming young strike prince of Portman Road, turned in a superbly executed effort to sink the mid-table Canaries.

It was a rallying performance from a Town team splattered with youth and promise that has been doing much better than results have indicated in the ringing out of the old year over the worrying past month or so.

Whatever has been lacking in the losing end to '84 it has certainly not been team spirit. This was evident yesterday as the Suffolk side fashioned a win that some of their followers had been thinking was never coming.

Norwich, a side that have chalked up some wonderful triumphs this season to thwart the title chasers, could have no complaints although they felt that a tackle by inspiring Town skipper Butcher at the start of the second-half on 36-year-old warhorse striker Channon should have brought a penalty.

It was a debatable decision but for once the rub of the green was with Ipswich and few could begrudge the struggling Town side three golden points to herald the New Year with this first home league win since October 20.

The showing of Dozzell, only a few weeks past his 17th birthday, was a delight and if this young brave's legs can keep pace with his beautiful football brain over the next few weeks what a boost it could be.

Playing against an England centre-half in Dave Watson and big money central defensive partner in Steve Bruce, how well the lad shaped up.

This lithe, gangling attacker who only left his schooldesk to begin his soccer apprenticeship six months ago had a hand in the ice-breaking first goal.

Cranson, a tower of strength alongside the cool and assured Osman at the heart of the Town defence, took a gigantic throw-in from the left not far from the corner flag. Butcher got his head to it and then Dozzell added his precise touch of the head that knocked the ball down to Gates who flashed home a timely shot from eight yards.

It was the first home league goal since Mark Brennan scored in the 75th minute of the 3-3 draw with Watford on November 3 and the Ipswich fans were doubly glad of it; pleased for the goal itself and delighted at the chance to beat out the bitter cold with their stamping, clapping and cheering.

The Dozzell goal was a real picture effort at the end of a lovely build-up.

Gates played to Putney on the right and the midfield battler, who got his fourth booking of the season in the 39th minute for a tackle from behind on Mendham, crossed to the left for Zondervan to plant a header at the feet of Dozzell who turned to rifle in a crisp right footer from 12 yards that flashed past Woods.

Cooper, who has been going through a shaky spell of late in the Ipswich goal, displayed plenty of safe and sound goalkeeping to thwart all that Norwich had to offer.

But the best chances were at the other end of the field to his goal as they have been in many of the recent defeats without being capitalised on for a variety of reasons.

Gates should have had his second goal of the game in the 72nd minute when he could have ended a personal league goal famine that stretches back to late October in double fashion.

Cranson pumped the ball upfield as he slid into a ferocious challenge. Dozzell, holding off Watson, slipped the ball sideways into the path of Gates who looked a good bet to go on and beat Woods.

But with the England senior squad 'keeper positioned perfectly Gates played the ball back into the path of Dozzell at a time when he probably wasn't expecting it.

Dozzell got in a left foot shot which Watson had to sweep away from near the line and the Canaries kept alive a glimmer of hope of saving the match.

Bruce had been booked for a 51st minute foul on Dozzell in a match full of good old fashioned local derby atmosphere and spirit on a difficult pitch being made more tricky all the time as heavy rain lashed down.

Butcher, again operating at left-back, snuffed out the right wing threat of the Whitton winger Donowa, who has made it into the big time with City.

What a great player Butcher is and it's no wonder that the no sale sign is still being flashed in the face of Manchester United manager Ron Atkinson despite the thought of a transfer fee that could ease the board's financial worries and leave money to spend on new talent.

The teams

IPSWICH: Cooper, Yallop, Butcher, Zondervan, Osman, Cranson, Putney, Brennan, Dozzell, McCall, Gates. Sub: Parkin.
NORWICH: Woods, Haylock, Downs, Bruce, Mendham, Watson, Devine, Channon, Deehan, Farrington (sub Gordon 70 mins), Donowa.
Referee: Mr. T. Bune (Berkshire).
Attendance: 21,710.

Dozzell superb for his age

RELIEVED Ipswich manager Bobby Ferguson said; "Today we made the good chances and finished them off. It was a grand all-round battling team performance."

The Town boss continued: "Jason Dozzell was superb for his age. Once he develops real First Division stamina he will be a hell of a player. But it all boils down to taking the chances and we did it today.

The windy conditions and tacky pitch did not help matters but the players overcame the conditions well and I was well pleased with all of them," continued Ferguson.

Of the "was it, wasn't it a penalty?" Butcher tackle on Channon remarked: "It could have gone one way or the other but it wasn't clear cut. Terry went for the ball but didn't clean him out."

Norwich boss Ken Brown thought otherwise and said: "I thought the referee missed a penalty there and I told him so but more than this I was not happy with the way my team were still asleep when Ipswich went into the lead.

"In the second-half we played a bit better than in the first but were always shaky on a day when Butcher did everything right and Donowa did nearly everything wrong.

"Dozzell was impressive for Ipswich who did not look like a struggling side. They have just not been getting the breaks," added Brown.

On the injury front Town manager Ferguson said that Brennan, whose performance he described as "superb", would now rest his groin injury for a day or two but should be fit for Saturday.

• **DOZZELL'S DAZZLER . . .** Ipswich Town's seventeen-year-old striker Jason Dozzell turns and fires home his 56th minute goal for his club in yesterday's local derby 2-0 win over Norwich City. The top picture shows how the young attacker who only left school in the summer gets the better of England international centre half Dave Watson. The middle picture sees the ball in the back of the net and City keeper Chris Woods on his knees while, below, skipper Terry Butcher leads the congratulations for the young hero. (Pictures by Richard Snasdell).

• **ERIC GATES** raises one finger in the direction of the main stand to signal his third minute goal that ended both his and Ipswich Town's home league goal famine. Joining in the celebrations are (left to right) Trevor Putney, Romeo Zondervan and Jason Dozzell.

I was dipped in and out of the first team after making my debut. A protective Bobby Ferguson tried to ease me in. Contributed by Roy Knightsbridge

In Milk Cup quarter-final action against QPR in January 1985. The day that I saw my brother Tony fighting on the pitch as I went to receive a throw-in. Newsquest

Being presented with Man of the Match champagne by Ipswich Town legend Ray Crawford in 1987. I can't believe I'm in the club's top-10 all-time goalscorers list alongside people like him. Newsquest

I was immensely proud to play for England at youth team level and gutted that a senior cap never followed. Contributed by Roy Knightsbridge

Celebrating one of my two goals against promotion rivals Derby County at Portman Road in March 1992. That was a big win. Newsquest

Held aloft by my brother Tony after a 1-1 draw at Oxford United clinched promotion in April 1992. Getty

10

A Negative Arena

AT THE end of my first full season of senior football I prepared for my PFA awards do debut. Those who had been before told me the agenda. All the heavies of the football world meet up in Covent Garden, you have an all-day piss up, go back to the hotel, have a shower, put your dinner suit on, look a million and then go to Grosvenor House to kick on again.

I didn't pace myself too well. I was only 17 and I was trying to keep up with all the older Ipswich boys. That was a schoolboy error. I went back to the hotel, spewed up everywhere multiple times, somehow pulled myself together, got my dickie bow on and did it all over again until about five o'clock in the morning.

That was how it was at every club back then. There was a drinking culture. It wasn't long before I started losing all of the things that had got me there in the first place. All that discipline started to dwindle. There were distractions.

I went into the 1985/86 season having got a few 'well done' comments from my peers and some adulation from the crowd. Gradually I started to feel like I belonged. I was still pretty reserved and quiet, but was gaining more and more confidence out of what I could do with the football.

Looking back, I now know I was a kid with a talent, but who wasn't psychologically ready. Who's your friend, who's not? There are people with agendas. You start getting paranoid. People were being nice to me. *What does he want?* You're trying to figure all this out. That went on for years.

I was on the bench for the opening game, but soon started against Manchester United, Tottenham and Liverpool. Now I'm playing against people like Bryan Robson, Frank Stapleton, Chris Waddle, Ossie Ardiles, Ian Rush and Alan Hansen week-in, week-out. This time there was no dipping out of the team for spells.

After the 1-0 home win against Spurs, Brian Scovell wrote in the *Daily Mail* that Bobby Ferguson was 'like a man who had just emerged from the maternity ward after watching the birth of his son'. Bobby was quoted as saying, 'Forget the hooligans and players on drink-driving charges, let's talk about football. Dozzell and Brennan are doing things that excite me and that's what the public want to see. We are continuing with our tradition here of producing our own youngsters. They are fresh-faced kids with clear minds and they don't worry about losing. They say, "Just give me the ball and let's play." They just want to express themselves. Dozzell and Brennan did a great job against Manchester United's Bryan Robson and Norman Whiteside in midweek [a 1-0 loss] and today they've dominated Ossie Ardiles and Mike Hazard.'

Mark Brennan was a couple of years older than me. He scored in my debut game against Coventry too and we both played for England under-21s. People ask if there was a sense of competition between us to be seen as 'the brightest young star' or whatever. I didn't see it that way. I was just trying to learn from everyone, including him. Two years is a big gap at that age. I wasn't filled out still, but he was by 18. Mark was a very good player – tough, two-footed, good engine. He had a good career, playing for Manchester City in the early '90s, but I'm surprised he didn't go right to the top.

The feelgood factor surrounding our new-look young team didn't last long. Liverpool battered us 5-0. A 3-0 home loss to Aston Villa brought the first chants of 'Ferguson out'. Ian Cranson, our England under-21 defender, made a couple of costly mistakes. We were all feeling the pressure.

There was a 12-game run without a win from mid-September to late November – ten of them ending in defeat. After a 4-3 defeat to Everton, we went 3-0 up against Oxford the following week only to lose 4-3 again as John Aldridge scored a hat-trick. That was really bad for morale.

It was during that period that my old youth team-mate Michael Cole scored on his full debut. I assisted him in a 2-2 home draw with Newcastle and we enjoyed our celebration together. He's another one I am gobsmacked didn't go higher. Michael had everything. When I first saw him as a schoolboy, I thought he was better than me. He ended up dropping down the divisions to play for Port Vale and Fulham, though.

Away from the pressure of the league, we did OK in the cups. After a 3-1 home win against Darlington in the Milk Cup, Bobby said, 'I was particularly pleased with the way Dozzell held the ball up and looked for the right people.

The young lad did well up front with [Alan] Sunderland and [Kevin] Wilson taking wide positions. It could well be that it will be his number one position.' I then scored a good solo goal in the second leg.

Dave Allard's report on the 2-0 win at Grimsby in the following round states, 'Dozzell's first half display was nothing short of superb with the friendly home crowd applauding lavishly some of the 17-year-old player's subtle skills that at times bamboozled the opposition.' You forget what it was like. Thankfully a lot of that stuff went over my head at the time otherwise my brain would have been fried. I was just enjoying playing football.

We smashed Swindon 6-1 in round four, while the league form picked up either side of Christmas. A 1-0 home win against QPR marked my 50th league appearance on the week of my 18th birthday. That's a lot of football by that age. I don't think that would happen now. Managers dip even the best young players in and out to look after them. Even Phil Foden, for example, didn't reach that milestone until he was 20 years and seven months old. I think it probably did contribute to me burning out towards the end of my career.

Liverpool eventually knocked us out of the Milk Cup in the fifth round, but against the odds we beat them in the league. After that came the conclusion to an FA Cup epic with West Ham. The first game had finished 0-0 at their place. I scored a really good goal to give us an extra-time lead in the replay at Portman Road, but they equalised and we faced each other again on Suffolk soil just two days later. Bobby Robson came to watch that third meeting, which we were unfortunate to lose 1-0 in extra time. Dave Allard wrote, 'The England boss is no doubt among the growing band of admirers of blossoming Town starlet Jason Dozzell who, over the past few games, has finally been taken to the hearts of some supporters who have often failed to appreciate the gifts of this remarkable Ipswich-born player who has only just turned 18.'

I'll talk about England in greater detail in the next chapter. Let's deal with my playing style here and how it wasn't everyone's cup of tea in the beginning. How would I describe my game? No stress. I played at my own pace. The aggressive side only started to develop when I was about 21. As you get older you learn how to tackle and use your arms and body more.

In those early years I was definitely languid and that could be portrayed as lazy. I knew I had to adapt and get a different rhythm in my play. I had to get a little bit quicker, a little less lackadaisical. That languid style had to turn into football arrogance when I had the ball. Out of possession I wasn't great, but I did enough.

I didn't want to just be seen as a luxury player who flits in and out and does what he wants. Yes, I had to be really good at the things I was good at, but I also knew I had to work on the other bits too. I had people like Romeo Zondervan and, later, George Williams, who could dig in and pass the ball to me. David Linighan arrived in '88 and was a hard player. I couldn't watch them all run around and get the tackles in and me not do it. I didn't want people thinking I wasn't putting it in, so I tried to look more proactive. I wanted that little bit of respect. Yeah, he can play, but he can get stuck in too. He's not going to go missing on a Tuesday night in Hull or Barnsley, or wherever. You can rely on him, he's a good character. That's the sort of praise I sought.

The other thing people ask is, 'What was your favourite position?' I don't really have an answer to that. My debut had been up front, but the next year I went into midfield and I ended up switching between the two positions. I didn't like long spells up front. I liked dipping in and out. That seemed to work for me. If I had a couple of months in midfield it would catch the opposition out when I went up front again.

After that FA Cup epic against West Ham, because of some postponements, we went on trips to Bahrain and Iraq to play their national sides. That seems an odd thing to do looking back. All I remember is how hot it was and there being lots of security people everywhere with guns. I guess there was some financial incentive to the club.

When the league action resumed, we ground out some 1-0 wins to stay in with a chance of beating the drop. At the end of April, we fought back from 2-0 down against Oxford in our final home game. I scored the equaliser and we won 3-2. We thought we were safe. After that though we lost to West Ham, who were going for the title, followed by Sheffield Wednesday. Oxford, unexpectedly, then beat Arsenal 3-0 a few days later. It meant we were relegated.

That was really painful. I cried like a baby, just like I had done in 1975 when I listened to us lose to West Ham in the FA Cup semi-final on the radio. I remember not doing anything for a few days. Nothing. Eighteen years in the top flight over. I felt guilty. I felt numb. *I've played my part in taking this great team down.* All sorts of things were going through my head. Very quickly, however, my mindset changed to, 'I have to get us back up.'

Terry Butcher went to Rangers. That hit me hard. Terry and Russell Osman had really looked after me and now they were both gone. I'd started off playing alongside my heroes, a team full of internationals, but they were all leaving and we were struggling. It was just the end of a cycle. Every club goes through them. We had all those great years and it was never going to last for ever. Again, I have to recognise that it was good for me personally. I would never have got the amount of games I did at that age if it wasn't for that rebuild. No chance.

There was a strong belief we'd bounce straight back, but life in the Second Division started with us failing to beat Grimsby and Oldham at home. The club started to have a bit of a dip and there was a lot of unrest. Crowds started to drop below 10,000.

We still ended up finishing fifth and faced Charlton in the play-off final. The first game, at Portman Road, ended 0-0. I had a good headed chance saved. We went 2-0 down in the second leg, at Selhurst Park, before Steve McCall pulled one back late on after Mich d'Avray's shot had come back off the post. There was still time for us to salvage the game. I produced a great turn, cut inside and bent a shot just around the post. That was that. Charlton went on to beat Leeds in the final.

I was devastated. Really down. Again, it was another lesson in how to feel the pain. I was starting to learn about the importance of not getting too high when you win and not too low when you lose. That's always what I tell my son Andre now. Football is not about when you're winning five- or six-nil, it's about how you handle pressure and disappointment. Because disappointment will come. That's a fact.

The board had reportedly given Bobby an ultimatum before that season started – get us promoted or your time is up. I don't know if that was true or not but, controversially, he became the first manager in the club's history to be fired.

There's no doubt that injuries and financial constraints had left Bobby fighting with one hand tied behind his back. The players weren't happy. Kevin Wilson was quoted as saying, 'Bobby has had to battle hard at the club in a very difficult time and I am very, very sad that he is leaving.' John Deehan said, 'When this happens to a manager you as a player feel partly to blame.' Paul Cooper was even more outspoken, saying, 'Nobody deserves to be put under the pressure Bob has had over the last six months. It's so unfair the way he has been treated.'

You can imagine how I felt. I was really upset. This was the man who put me in the record books. It took a brave man to put a schoolboy in. We'd just lost to lower-division Shrewsbury in the FA Cup and there was a lot of pressure on Bobby at that time. Do you really go and pick a schoolboy to get you out of trouble? Not really. What had he seen in me to take that gamble? It wasn't until years later that I realised the magnitude of what he'd done.

My next thought was, 'Bobby liked me, will the new manager?' I was in the real world now.

John Duncan came in from Third Division club Chesterfield to become only the eighth manager in Ipswich's history. Paul Cooper, Steve McCall and Kevin Wilson were the latest senior players to depart. Now we had a *really* young team. A 17-year-old Chris Kiwomya emerged from the youth team. I was still only 19, as were Dalian Atkinson, Chris O'Donnell and Neill Rimmer. Then you had the likes of Mark Brennan, Jon Hallworth, Frank Yallop, Ian Cranson, Mick Stockwell, David Lowe, Michael Cole, Neil Wood and Tony Humes all in their early 20s. Through the spine of the team you always need experience and we simply didn't have it.

There was some speculation at that time, given the club's financial issues, that either me or Mark Brennan would have to be sold. Nothing was ever said to me, though, and I never gave it a moment's thought. I was sure that if one of us were to go it would be Mark first because he was more advanced. In the end, both of us stayed.

All of a sudden, I was getting towards the top of the tree. I was hailed as the new best thing. Jason's a wonder kid. Jason's a boy wonder. People were expecting a lot and those expectations swamped me for a bit. I slowed down. I found it tough. I was lacking in certain areas, with my personality, dealing with certain things away from the field. You're naive to all that at 16 and 17, but as you get a little bit older you become more aware of pressure. I'd say it was once I'd become fully established in the team that those feelings kicked in.

I had to figure out how to deal with that on my own. How do I get to the next level? What are you supposed to eat? How much sleep am I supposed to get? For a while I couldn't raise a gallop. I was eating steak the night before the game in the hotel, which my body then couldn't digest. I was having too much bread in the morning. I just felt lethargic. Trying to manage all that was hard. Gradually, over time, I started to speak to people, work all that out and felt a lot better.

Personally, I loved John Duncan. After every game, him, me, John Wark (when he had returned for his second spell), David Linighan and BBC Suffolk commentator Bryan Knights would be in the Ipswich Arms having a beer and chatting about the game. He was just one of the lads. That's another thing you'd never get these days.

John was always good to me, but his ideology wasn't a great fit for my style. We were 4-4-2 every week. It would be a case of get the ball to Frank Yallop, big diagonal to Mich d'Avray, Mich knocks it down for David Lowe and then we're just scrapping about for the loose ball. Two-v-two in the middle, win your battle, that's it. No playing through the lines, no dropping into pockets.

I've always said that once you cross that white line you have to make your own decisions. You've got to believe what you believe in. If it doesn't come off then you'll get bollocked and possibly dropped, but at least you were true to yourself.

I would not be stereotyped into John's way of football. I couldn't. I trained the way he wanted during the week, but then did what I thought was right for the team once the game got under way. I got frustrated if I was hardly touching the ball, so when I thought it was the right time for us to try and take the game by the scruff of the neck I would just go and take it off the centre-halves and trust myself. I knew if I got caught out playing that way then I was in trouble. But that was the Ipswich style I'd grown up watching. If you don't want that then drop me. I never had that conversation with John, though. I was always waiting for him to say something to me about not following instructions, but he would always be complimentary. It was weird.

* * *

Dalian Atkinson came down from Telford when he was 15 and used to come and stay at my house a lot. He became a really good friend.

Like me, Dalian was a skinny little kid. Unlike me, he had unbelievable pace. He came back one pre-season built like a brick shithouse – absolutely massive, muscles everywhere. His development was rapid. I'd never seen anything like it before or since.

To start with he was raw, but eventually he honed his talent. Towards the end of John Duncan's first season he scored the best hat-trick I've ever seen in an Ipswich shirt against Middlesbrough. He was ridiculously explosive that day. The power in those shots was frightening. It was just a phenomenal performance.

I had a lot of fun times with Dalian. Boy, he was a larger-than-life character. I was a choirboy compared to him. He lived like he played – fast. He had the fastest cars and drove them to their limits. He'd do the 50-odd miles from Brentwood to Ipswich in about 30 minutes. I'm not joking. I'd be in the front holding on for dear life, watching the speed dial go up and up and up. You couldn't say anything to him, though.

One time, Dalian drove me and Chris Kiwomya up to Sheffield in his Porsche 911. I made the point that Chris should give me the seat in the front because I was the tallest. He wasn't having it. We argued and I lost. In the end I was the one wedged in that little bit behind the front two seats. Peeping between the two front headrests, I was soon watching the clock go up in the blink of an eye – 40, 50, 60. That was not a fun journey.

Another Dalian story involves pre-season. Whenever the club said 'we're going to Sweden this summer' the lads were doing cartwheels. We loved Scandinavia. It was vibrant, lively as anything and the standard of girls was unreal. Those trips ended up more like stag weeks. It was running, drinking, playing, drinking on repeat. We'd all be sneaking back into the rooms late at night. Pete Trevivian, my old youth coach who'd been promoted to a first-team role, caught us a few times, but he was a good guy and didn't say anything to John Duncan.

One night we went to a nightclub on a boat. Nigel Gleghorn got in an argument with a local and this guy, bizarrely, ended up karate chopping Nigel in the belly. Just as I was processing that image, out of nowhere Dalian came charging down the boat's gangway and launched himself into an Eric Cantona-style kung-fu kick. With two feet off the floor he crashed straight into this bloke's chest. We all quickly scarpered after that!

I couldn't believe it when Chris Kiwomya called me in 2016 to say Dalian had died. When he told me, 'Jason, the police kicked his head in,' I thought that was an exaggeration. But he was right. They did. They tasered him and left lace marks on his head. That's a hard one to get your head around.

A bit like me, things weren't going to plan for Dalian post playing career. His mental health wasn't in a good place. Seeing what happened to him was another motivation to do this book. Everyone has their struggles. I'll talk about mine in due course.

* * *

I don't know what more I can say about that period at Ipswich. A great era had ended. Supporters weren't happy with the style we were playing and the direction the club was going in. It was just a negative arena.

It was a frustrating time really. We missed out on the play-offs three years in a row, finishing eighth, eighth and ninth. Crowds dwindled. When it's like that, decisions have to be made. Ultimately, John Duncan got the sack and I had another manager to impress.

11

Man Overboard

MY PROGRESSION with England was as rapid as it was with Ipswich.

Two months after my debut goal at Portman Road, I was called up to the England under-17 squad. We went away for a friendly tournament in Cannes and I scored on my international debut – a 4-0 win against Mexico.

Six months later, still 16, I had moved up to the under-18s. Guess what, I scored on my debut for them too. That was in a 5-3 win against Iceland, at Manchester City's Maine Road, as part of European Championship qualifying.

A couple of years later, in September 1986, I made my England under-21s debut aged 19. No goal this time. In fact, I was subbed off as we drew 1-1 in Östersund, Sweden. My old Essex nemesis Tony Adams scored in that game.

In those days the England senior team and under-21s played the same fixtures and travelled together. Terry Butcher – who just a few months earlier had been a central figure in the 1986 World Cup in Mexico – had recently transferred to Rangers, but was back down in Suffolk at the time of that international weekend. He suggested it made sense for us to travel to Luton airport together.

I met Butch at Portman Road in the early hours of the morning and he said, 'Do you fancy driving?' There was a problem. I hadn't got my contact lenses in. I was still getting used to them and I didn't like having them in when I wasn't playing. I was too scared to tell Terry that, though. I was this shy kid in awe of him. He was like my surgeon and my doctor. If he says something, I do it. 'Yeah, no problem, I'll drive,' was therefore my reply. 'Mr Magoo' was at the wheel.

Sod's law, there was thick fog. Thankfully my high-value passenger soon went to sleep as I leant forward squinting into the gloom. Every time I got near a roundabout I hit the brakes sharp and he'd sit bolt upright. 'It's all right Butch, just a bit of a heavy foot, sorry, go back to sleep.' That went on all the way to Luton airport. I was so relieved when we finally pulled into the car park.

On the plane there was a hierarchy. The big boys sat at the front, us kids were in the middle and then you had the media at the back. Once we were up in the air, I felt a tap on my shoulder. Butch was stood in the aisle. 'Come on Jason, let me introduce you to a few people.' He took me to go and meet Bryan Robson, Peter Shilton, John Barnes, Mark Bright – all these big, big names. That was just a lovely touch. He didn't have to do that. Russell Osman, as I've said, was another one who looked out for me back then. I love them both for how they treated me when I was young and I love them for how they still treat me today.

I played a couple more times for the under-21s that season. One trip to Spain sticks in my mind. Bobby Robson's men had won 4-2 thanks to Barcelona striker Gary Lineker scoring four times at the home ground of Real Madrid and we'd won 2-1 thanks to goals from Tony Cottee and David Rocastle. Spirits were high on that journey home.

In the summer of 1987, there wasn't much time for me to dwell on Ipswich's play-off heartache against Charlton because a week later I was going away with England – this time for the prestigious Toulon Tournament.

That was the first time Paul Gascoigne was in the squad. My first impressions of him, you won't be surprised to hear, were that he was great fun. Daft as a brush, as Sir Bobby once said, but a heart of gold. Then training started. Wow. Everything about him was unbelievably good – dribbling, strength, pace, fleet-footed, change of direction. He had that football arrogance. Even if he was marked, he'd be demanding the ball. I played with and against some top young players, but he was undoubtedly the best.

We played France in a group game. They beat us 2-0, David Ginola got both and he was unbelievable. France went on to win it and he got named Player of the Tournament. It was no surprise to me to see him do so well for Newcastle and Tottenham in the Premier League a few years down the line.

The likes of Cláudio Taffarel and Hristo Stoichkov – Brazil and Bulgaria legends in the making – also starred in that tournament. We finished fifth after beating Portugal on penalties. It was a great experience but, unfortunately, it ended on a real sour note thanks to stupidity on my behalf.

My sister lived in Italy at that time working as a model. She came over to France and joined us for dinner towards the end of the trip. We all went down to the marina one afternoon. It was beautiful. The drinks went down well in the sunshine. That's when things escalated.

Tootie eventually went back to the hotel and our big group fractured into smaller numbers. I was left with my Ipswich team-mate Mark Brennan and Norwich duo Robert Rosario and Dale Gordon. I had to put my Norwich hatred to one side when away with England. To be fair, Robert and Dale were good lads. Dale, in particular, was a funny guy.

Staggering back along the marina, our little East Anglian party decided to climb aboard this unattended fancy-looking boat. That soon turned into us egging each other on to jump across on to the next boat along. Boat-to-boat we hopped until we were greeted with a fairly sizeable gap. One by one the other three all just about made it. Then it was my turn. *Splash!* Man overboard!

The cold water sobered me up quick. *That wasn't the smartest thing to do.* But it was late at night and no one was about. 'Phew,' I thought. 'Looks like I've got away with it.' Dripping wet, the other boys giggling away, I tip-toed back through the hotel reception, up the stairs and back along the corridor to my room.

The issue was that our team hotel overlooked the marina. Little did I know that Dave Sexton, our manager, had heard the commotion, woken up and looked out of his window. The next morning, we all got pulled in for an emergency meeting. I was nervous. Dave had managed Chelsea and Manchester United and led England to two UEFA Under-21 Championship titles. I liked him, but knew he had a tough side.

'I know what happened last night,' he said, looking out across the room. 'It was too dark for me to see the culprits, but I saw one with bandy legs running away from the scene.' He demanded the guilty person own up, but I kept my head down and so did the other lads. In training that day I was walking around stiff as a board, trying to keep my knees together! I thought I'd got away with it, but the national newspapers somehow found out what had gone on and published a story naming the four of us. A disappointed Dave sent us all home early.

I had to wait 14 months until I was selected for the under-21s again and the call-ups were sporadic after that. Ipswich being outside of the top flight probably didn't help my cause, but neither did my behaviour on that trip.

When the England trips did briefly return they proved financially useful to me. We replicated the high-stakes card schools we'd seen the senior lads involved in at our clubs. Three card brag was the big game at that time. On the planes, coaches, in the hotel rooms – everyone played it, and I was pretty good at it. On one outbound trip I won about three grand, which made playing together the next day slightly awkward.

Paul Merson once owed me £500. We'd give each other cheques in those days, but Paul's kept bouncing. Eventually it did go through. The same can't be said for another player, who I won't name. He ended up owing me about a grand, but I couldn't get hold of him for love nor money after that.

Further down the line, when I was at Tottenham, we had some big games. I'm talking £40 or £50 blind bets. Sometimes you'd end up with two grand in one pot. I saw players lose about four, five grand and then the next day they had got to go and play football together. You knew what you were getting into, though.

Playing for Ipswich, my hometown club, was magic. But it had robbed me of my football fandom. Supporting England gave me that outlet. I loved cheering them on.

In 1990, when David Pleat's wondrous volley helped see off Belgium in the last 16 of the World Cup, I was enthralled. After the subsequent quarter-final win against Cameroon, I gave Terry Butcher a call and pleaded, 'Any chance you can get us some tickets?' I thought it was a long shot but, Terry being Terry, he sorted it out.

John Duncan had just been sacked as Ipswich manager and replaced by John Lyall. Against the backdrop of that, me, Tony and two mates set off from Ipswich on our little adventure. We drove all the way in my Vauxhall Astra, stopping off on the way to visit my sister in Milan, before going on to Turin. There were some scary mountain roads to navigate along the way with sheer drops to the side. All in all, the journey took about 17 hours, but we got there in the end.

Eventually we got to the England hotel, but it was behind a secure gate guarded by police. Tony marched up first and I saw a few officers' hands slowly start to move towards their guns. I soon came bounding on to the scene thinking I could fix the situation. Talking in that awkward way English people do when abroad, I raised my voice, adopted a ridiculous Italian accent and gestured with my hands. 'Four ticketos! Semi-final! Terry Butcher!' They just stared at us with a half-irritated, half-pitying expression that suggested we weren't the first English idiots they'd had to deal with that day.

This went on for 45 minutes or so. Luckily, one of the England staff eventually came out. I shouted at them to come over, explained the situation and they went back in and got the tickets off Butch for us. He'd come good on his promise.

We watched the game. It was heartbreaking to see Gazza's tears and the penalty shoot-out defeat. I really thought we were going to win that tournament. There were police vans everywhere afterwards. The army came in. You couldn't move. Then I had the long journey home to contemplate working under a new manager and another season outside the top flight.

About a week later I went out and left that Vauxhall Astra parked at Ipswich nightclub Hollywoods overnight. I went to watch Tony play Sunday morning football for Kitcheners the next day, saw a burnt-out car behind the goal and thought nothing of it. Then a policeman came over to me. 'Do you know that's your car?' 'What? No, no, that can't be mine.' 'Yes, we've checked the plate, it's your car.' It turned out someone had nicked my car from Hollywoods and left it burnt out at the exact place I was going the next morning. How's your luck?!

They obviously thought it was dodgy. They thought I'd done it on purpose. 'Watch out, this might be fraud,' was what they were thinking. I guess it was the obvious conclusion. Even my mates were saying, 'You haven't, have you?' No! It was just coincidence. Thankfully I did end up getting the insurance money. Stuff like that just seems to happen to me.

As much as I loved supporting England, I obviously dreamed of playing for them too. On that drive back from Turin, was I allowing myself to think about the possibility of earning senior international caps? Definitely. I was getting picked two years above my age group for the under-21s.

Someone from the USA international setup did contact me at one stage, having been made aware of my heritage, asking if I'd be interested in playing for them. It turned out that wasn't actually possible because the rules back then were that you couldn't switch nations after representing someone at youth level. Regardless, my answer would have been a respectful 'no' because I very much had my sights set on playing for England.

I did get pretty close to realising that dream. In my final year at Ipswich, during a period when we were doing well in the inaugural Premier League, John Lyall kept saying, 'They're watching you, you're close.' I was on standby once, but it didn't happen.

Looking back, I am disappointed by that. Let's be honest, that wasn't a great era for England. We didn't qualify for the '94 World Cup. I don't want to name names, but Graham Taylor picked people who were nowhere near as good as me in a pure football sense. Maradona, Platini and Zico were celebrated number tens in Argentina, France and Brazil, but England refused to move on from a rigid 4-4-2 system and just didn't trust technical and flair players like other nations did.

I'm not putting myself in that bracket, by the way. You can say that about players a lot more talented than me. Glenn Hoddle, John Barnes, Paul Gascoigne, Paul Merson – did we really get the best out of them? Then Hoddle got the England job himself and even he didn't select people like Gascoigne and Matt Le Tissier.

Nowadays, of course, things have changed. It's great seeing the likes of Jack Grealish, Phil Foden and James Maddison getting the chance to express themselves for the Three Lions.

Might I have sneaked a cap or two had our nation's attitude to the game been a bit more forward-thinking back in the '90s? Perhaps. But, as would become a recurring theme throughout my career, I didn't help myself.

12

Promotion and the Premier League

I RETURNED from my World Cup escapade in Turin ready for a new chapter in my career. Having been Bobby Ferguson's golden child and part of John Duncan's post-match drinking club, I was wondering whether my good run with managers was about to come to an end. The mood surrounding the club wasn't good and I fully expected a new man to come in with the intention of shaking things up.

Those fears were immediately ended when I had my first meeting with John Lyall. As soon as he saw me his first words were, 'I've got you at last.' *What?* Incredibly, he'd remembered me from my Langham Lions days. Straight away I felt a million dollars.

John's first season in charge ended with a 14th-place finish, the club's lowest since the mid-'60s. Going into the 1991/92 season, you could sense that apathy had overtaken anger among the fanbase.

This was season number six outside of the top flight for a club that not so long ago had been part of Europe's elite and the recent league positions suggested things were going to get worse, not better. To say no one saw what was coming is therefore a major understatement.

I scored our opening goal of that season. We went 3-0 up at Twerton Park, but a Bristol Rovers side containing impressive teenager Marcus Stewart came roaring back in the last half hour to draw 3-3. Supporters must have been thinking 'here we go again'. After that setback, a crowd of less than 9,000 turned up for our home opener against Port Vale and we scraped a 2-1 win thanks to Neil Thompson's penalty.

After a decent enough August and September, we stuttered into Christmas. Just two wins from 16 games saw us exit both the League Cup and Full Members' Cup and sit somewhere in mid-table. It wasn't going well. John was under pressure.

A 2-0 Boxing Day home win against Charlton, Chris Kiwomya with both goals, turned the tide, though. I got the winner against Blackburn at Portman Road a few days later and then we really clicked into gear, gaining some powerful momentum.

By this point in my Ipswich career, I'd become well embedded in the game's drinking culture. I'd progressed from the shy kid having the odd drink with his heroes for a bit of Dutch courage, to regularly having a few pints after the match, to now being at the heart of a midweek drinking club. Every Wednesday, six or seven of us would meet in The Swan after training and go right through, ending up at Hollywoods. The core members were me, David Linighan, Chris Kiwomya and Warky.

Training on Thursday morning was always hard work. Most of us would do just enough to get through the session, but David Linighan would put a black bin bag on underneath his kit and run around like a madman to sweat all the alcohol out. After that, we'd all go home, have a long sleep and come back bright as a button on Friday in preparation for the game. That was the pattern.

There were only two times I went out the night before a game. The first was on New Year's Eve in 1989. Chris Kiwomya and I went for a few down the local and we got beat 5-0 at Port Vale the next day. John Duncan went nuts and we both got fined. Two years later we had Port Vale on New Year's Day again. What did Chris and I do? Yep, we went out on New Year's Eve again. Only until midnight for a couple, to be fair. We won 2-1 the next day – Chris got both goals and I got named man of the match. John Lyall had to dish out the fine this time, but he couldn't really go mad.

David Linighan, the captain, pulled me and Chris aside in training that week, looked us in the eyes all serious and said, 'You idiots.' We looked at the floor and mumbled, 'Sorry skip.' Then, after a dramatic pause, he added, 'You could have invited me!' We fell about laughing. That's a prime example of the camaraderie that group had.

There were six straight league wins from the middle of January to the end of March. We were a close-knit group who all knew our jobs. We gelled more and more as the games went on. We just got better and better. Don't get me wrong, it certainly wasn't like watching current-day Manchester City or anything like that. We just knew how to win games.

We had a lot of good people and good characters in that dressing room. There were relationships all over the park. Chris

Kiwomya had come into the team at 18 and was prominent up front. We were mates off the pitch and combined well on it. He was quick and I knew exactly when he was going to run in behind.

Johnny Wark, the man I had watched at close quarters growing up, arriving on the edge of the box to score time and time again, had returned to the club that summer from Middlesbrough. At 34 years old, he moved into defence and just cruised it back there because of his experience and ability to read the game. Alongside him, David Linighan was someone who would get busted up for you. He'd put his head in where it hurts. When it came to tough away games in the middle of November he was the man.

Neil Thompson was a brilliant left-back. He was strong and could score a goal with that powerful shot he possessed. Neil had a brilliant relationship with Steve Whitton. Steve was a 6ft 3in right-winger and we used that. When I saw that big diagonal from Neil to Steve flying through the air I was already making a run from midfield to pick up the knock-down.

Craig Forrest, my old youth team-mate, was in goal. He was a brilliant shot-stopper, a great commander of his box and saved us a bucketload of points. Simon Milton came in from non-league Bury Town and did incredibly well. He just strode straight into our dressing room. We also had Romeo Zondervan in midfield. I loved playing with him. He did more than his fair share of running, winning the ball and giving it to me. I needed that destroyer to help me out.

Paul Goddard was a very clever player. If it wasn't for injuries then Gavin Johnson could have been a top, top player.

Frankie Yallop was a brilliant right-back and a funny guy. Mick Stockwell, an academy graduate who went on to play more than 500 games for the club, had a vital role. Steve Palmer came in when he was needed, while centre-back Phil Whelan arrived later in the season and scored a couple of really important goals late on. The likes of Eddie Youds, David Gregory and Glenn Pennyfather all played their parts too.

We didn't have the best players in the division, but we had the best manager. That's what got us up. Tactically, John Lyall was so sharp. His attention to detail on the opposition was superb. And he was also a great man-manager whose door was always open. You wanted to play for him and go that extra yard for him. He was fantastic, he really was.

Around February time I played up front for a spell and scored four goals in three games, including two in a 5-2 home win against Portsmouth. Darren Anderton, who later became my Tottenham team-mate, got two that day but we were just too good for them.

After that we drew 0-0 with Liverpool at Portman Road in the FA Cup fifth round and, ten days later, travelled up to Anfield for a Wednesday night reply. We went 1-0 down, but Gavin Johnson scored a late equaliser and I then put us ahead in extra time, scoring at the second attempt after Bruce Grobbelaar had saved my initial one-on-one chance. I really, really enjoyed that goal – you can tell in my celebration. A minute after that though I dived in on Steve McManaman, and Jan Mølby thundered home the subsequent free kick from nowhere near where the foul had taken place. Not long afterwards, McManaman scored himself and we'd been knocked out. Still, it had been an exciting night and Liverpool manager Graeme Souness heaped praise on us, saying we'd be a credit to the First Division if we went up.

During the second half of that season my brother was in full flow. I'd be getting 25 tickets at a time for Tony and my mates and they'd make a weekend of every away game. More often than not I'd join them. Buzzing off a win, I'd declare in the dressing room, 'I'm not coming back on the coach with you lot, my brother and his friends are here, we're going out.' If we played in Liverpool, I stayed in Liverpool. If we played in London, I stayed in London. You get the picture.

Those nights were never by design, they were always spontaneous. One time I stayed in Birmingham and told my wife that my car had broken down. 'OK, just get home safe,' she said. Got away with that one, I thought. The next week we were back in Birmingham and my car actually did break down for real! That's karma for you. I had to bring the paperwork home as proof.

David Linighan got injured at the end of March. We were all gutted for him because he'd played such a big part in setting up the promotion push. It must have been so hard for him watching on from the sidelines. I wouldn't wish that on anybody, but it did give me the proudest moment of my career. I couldn't believe it when John Lyall pulled me to one side and said I was going to be captain for the last ten games. John Wark was the logical choice to take the armband, but John Lyall saw something in me to take on that role at such an important time.

He trusted me, and when someone does that you have to react. I had to change a bit personality-wise. I was a bit out of my comfort zone in team talks before the game, to be honest. I just spoke about how much it meant to the fans and how we couldn't let this slip now we were this close, things like that. On the pitch, I tried to lead by example by wanting the ball and giving everything. For some people, the extra responsibility of being captain can detract from their own performance, but it went the other way with me. That huge show of belief gave me extra confidence and discipline. I started taking more care about where and when I went out. It was a masterstroke from John. That's the art of management, knowing what buttons to press with different players.

Towards the end of March, I got both goals in a 2-1 home win against a Derby side who were up there with us. We went top of the table with that result and from then on in Ipswich fans were well and truly back. The whole place just had a great, great feel about it. The supporters got us over the line.

It was in that same game against Derby that I made one of my best ever tackles. John Lyall told me, 'There's a guy in the other team called George Williams and he's going to try and kick you early doors. Make sure you get him first.' So I launched into this tackle, two feet up, studs up, and cleaned him out. These days people would be calling for a ten-game ban it was so X-rated, but somehow I didn't get booked. I felt great after. I was thinking, 'I'm a hard man.' Me and George, who became my team-mate that summer, still talk about that today.

Newcastle was an iconic match. We were 2-0 down to Gavin Peacock's brace, but came back to win 3-2. Then, after a little four-game wobble, we drew 1-1 at Oxford to seal promotion.

Six years earlier I had vowed, as a 19-year-old, to get Ipswich Town my club – back in the big time. Now here I was, aged 24, having made good on that promise. Not only that, I'd got us over the line as the skipper. My brother came on the pitch and got me on his shoulders. I was just over the moon.

The beers were flowing on the journey home as cars honked their horns and flags hung from bridges on the motorways. Then we all went straight to Alan Brazil's pub, the Black Adder. It was full of Ipswich fans and we had a great time. Everyone was dancing on tables and on the bar – it was bedlam. Then it was on to Hollywoods nightclub. I don't think I slept at all. I had a quick shower in the morning, got my suit on, got on the bus, did the promotion parade and then we kicked on again after that.

Standing on the Town Hall balcony looking out at all those happy fans was so emotional for me. Memories of being out in that crowd looking up at my heroes in '78 and '81 came rushing back. It was a crazy, surreal, brilliant couple of days and, without doubt, the happiest time of my football career.

Winning the title secured us a place in the inaugural Premier League, a freshly branded top division that had broken away from the Football League after striking a multi-million-pound television deal with Sky. There was a cheesy advert with a player from each of the 22 teams working out in the gym and running down the tunnel together. Warky was our representative. The tagline was 'it's a whole new ball game'. Looking back, it was a monumental moment for English football, but at the time it didn't feel like a big deal.

Not for me anyway. I was just excited to be back in the top division and preparing to face all the big teams on a regular basis again.

Incredibly, we started the 1992/93 season with an eight-game unbeaten run. Granted, six of them ended in draws – including successive stalemates against Manchester United, Liverpool and Tottenham – but we had proven Souness right. We were ready to compete with the best.

It was in the final game of that unbeaten streak, a 2-1 home win against Wimbledon, that an incident occurred which had ramifications for years to come.

I was sandwiched between Vinnie Jones and John Fashanu at a corner. That was any player's worst nightmare. I knew what was coming and all I could think was, 'Please no, not the face, I'm going out later on.' My party plans were of no concern to the Crazy Gang, though. Vinnie caught me with an elbow. *Bang!* I went down like a sack of spuds. But he went down as well. Smart. He made out like he had been punched. The referee didn't know what to do.

My lip swelled up like a balloon. My brother took one look at me after the game and went marching straight over to Vinnie in the players' lounge. I feared the worst with two characters like that coming together and locking horns. It was threatening to all kick off, but thankfully they realised there were lots of children about and calmed down.

Tony is not one to forgive and forget, though. He held that grudge all the way through my career. He had words with Vinnie after Tottenham played Wimbledon the next season. He had more words at the PFA Player of the Year Awards.

He was always going up to him, squaring up. Those two just kept colliding.

Our good form continued. We put Aston Villa out of the League Cup and then, just before Christmas, we went to Carrow Road for a game against our bitter rivals. Mike Walker's men, like us, had made a surprisingly good start and were right up there too. The game was on TV and the stakes were high. We went 1-0 up early in the second half when I glanced on a corner and Chris Kiwomya headed in. Then, with two minutes to go, after they'd thrown everything at us, I clipped a ball forwards, Steve Whitton cushioned it down with his chest and Neil Thompson rifled in on the angle.

That was Norwich's first home defeat of the season. A few of our fans ran on the pitch in celebration. I felt someone behind me put a bobble hat on my head and give me a hug. I didn't know it at the time, but it was Tony. Anyway, I forgot I had this hat on and played on for a good couple of minutes before the referee said, 'Take that thing off, you idiot!'

After Christmas we beat Blackburn 2-1 at Portman Road and, come the start of 1993, we'd only lost twice. Confidence was sky high. Champions elect Manchester United came to Suffolk in late January. Schmeichel, Parker, Bruce, Pallister, Irwin, Sharpe, Ince, McClair, Giggs, Cantona, Hughes, Kanchelskis – their players rolled off the tongue. Alex Ferguson's men were sweeping everyone aside and drawing big crowds wherever they went, but we beat them 2-1. Schmeichel made a mistake for Chris Kiwomya's opener, I set up Frank Yallop for a rare goal and, after Brian McClair pulled one back, Clive Baker made a point-blank save from

Mark Hughes and we clung on to move within five points of the leaders.

Fourth in the Premier League, quarter-finals of the FA Cup, quarter-finals of the League Cup – we were in dreamland. Sadly, that proved to be the peak of our season. We went on a horrendous run after that and couldn't win a game for a good three or four months. The bubble had burst. I think teams worked us out. We were no longer the surprise package.

Sheffield Wednesday and Arsenal knocked us out of the League Cup and FA Cup respectively after quarter-final replays, while we tumbled down the league during a 13-game winless streak. The wheels well and truly fell off.

With three games to go we hosted Norwich. They had maintained their good form to stay at the top end of the table, while we were very much under the threat of relegation.

I was always quiet in the changing room before games and would do my own thing. When Norwich came along, though, I was vocal. I felt like I was representing every single one of our fans in the ground on derby days because I had been one of them when I was a kid. I put it upon myself to get the boys going for those games. I used to warn the players, 'My brother will be waiting outside if we lose.'

I scored the opener, which was a bit of a gift after Bryan Gunn missed the ball, but Chris Sutton, newly converted to a striker, headed them level before half-time. After the restart, Mick Stockwell stabbed us back in front before I sealed the win with a low, long-range shot. It took a few bobbles on a bad pitch, but I didn't care! I didn't get many from outside the box and this one had come against that lot up the road. Apart from that Milk Cup semi-final in 1985, I had a really good record against Norwich and was very proud of that.

In February there had been dreams of cup glory and European qualification, but we ended up surviving by the skin of our teeth. I went off on my summer holidays only thinking about how we could kick on next season. Little did I know it at the time, but it would be more than four years before I played for Ipswich Town again.

13

'The Next Hoddle'

I THOUGHT I was going to be at Ipswich for ever, right up until the day before I left.

I started renegotiating my contract with the club after the 1992/93 season ended. Before the Bosman ruling came into play in '95, talks would often start quite close to a deal expiring as clubs had more protection. I'd consistently given John Lyall the impression that I would never leave because that was honestly how I felt. We weren't that far away from sorting something out.

Then, in late July, with the big kick-off just a couple of weeks away, we went off on a pre-season trip to Finland. I was looking forward to the usual Scandinavian shenanigans.

While over there, one day, completely out of the blue, I took a phone call. 'Hi Jason, do you fancy a move?' said the voice on the other end. 'Sorry, what? Who are you?' 'My name's Steve Waggott, I hear you are out of contract, do you fancy a move?'

That caught me completely by surprise. 'Look, I'm not signing anything with you,' I said. 'But by all means go away and find out if there's any interest.' I was happy at Ipswich, but I knew my stock was high. From a pure ego point of view, I was intrigued to know whose radar I was on. I thought it could strengthen my hand in contract negotiations with Ipswich too. There was certainly no harm in finding out.

Twenty minutes later he called me back and said, 'Tottenham want to sign you.' *OK.* 'And Ossie wants to meet you tomorrow.' *Right.*

Now he'd really got my attention. Remember me wearing that Argentina shirt to Ipswich training as a kid? Ossie Ardiles was someone I had idolised when watching the World Cup in 1978. I knew my football history. I watched the 1981 FA Cup Final when Tottenham beat Manchester City after a replay. It was Ricky Villa, Glenn Hoddle and Ossie in that midfield and the way they played mesmerised me. After that, Tottenham were my second team.

Looking back, I was so naive. I just got on the plane the next day, didn't tell anybody, and went and met this complete stranger. He then took me to meet Ossie at the Swallow Hotel in Waltham Abbey.

In my mind I was going there just to listen to what they had to say and have a think, but before I knew it we were talking terms. The deal sounded great. Four-year contract, four and a half grand a week when I'd been negotiating for three and a half at Ipswich, a 100 grand signing-on fee, plus a car and a hotel for six months. I can't lie and say that the money side of it wasn't a big part of the appeal. It was.

By the end of that persuasive meeting, swept up in the excitement of it all, I'd agreed to the move. I woke up the next morning in a state of shock. *What the hell just happened?* I'd left Ipswich Town. I'd left my hometown club who I'd grown up supporting. I'm not ashamed to admit there were tears. I felt awful. I felt empty.

A fee of £1.9m was subsequently decided at a tribunal, which was a lot back then. For context, Roy Keane's £3.75m move from Nottingham Forest to Manchester United was the biggest deal of that summer.

I can't believe I didn't speak to John Lyall, my family or anyone about it. That was typical me; easily led and never switched on to who had my best interests at heart. Look, maybe conversations with others would have led to me signing for Tottenham anyway. As much as I loved Ipswich, I did have my career to think about. I was knocking on the door of the England squad and there was a World Cup in the USA, my dad's home nation, coming up. Tottenham were and are a big club. They'd just finished eight places above Ipswich in the league.

I'll never know how things would have panned out had I taken more time to think things through. What I do know now is that I was a vulnerable young man who was taken advantage of.

I got stung by Steve Waggott. In those days you paid your representative out of your signing-on fee, not your basic wage. I didn't know that, though. He was clever and organised a big signing-on fee rather than a big basic. Me being my usual naive self didn't question any of it. This guy had worked for me for one day – one day! – and suddenly he was asking me to transfer 30 grand to this bank account in Holland. It was crazy. I probably should have taken my brother to see him and said, 'Here's £500, you're not getting anything else,' but I paid up. At the end of the day, it was completely my fault for not being switched on and checking the details.

When doing some research for this book, I found that there's an almost identical story in Andy Cole's autobiography where he talks about Steve popping up out of nowhere and jumping on his move from Bristol City to Newcastle in that same summer of 1993, also demanding that very same figure – 30 grand. At the time of writing, Steve is the chief executive of Blackburn Rovers, having previously held the same position at Charlton, Coventry and Gillingham. There's an interview online where he describes himself as 'empathetic, loyal and transparent'. I'll say no more.

After being unveiled as a Tottenham player I spoke to the press. I told them exactly what I've just told you – that I wanted to be like Glenn Hoddle growing up and that I'd always had a soft spot for Spurs. My heart sank when I saw the headlines in the papers the next day. 'Dozzell: I've always supported Tottenham' and 'Dozzell: I can be the next Hoddle'.

I was quoted as saying, 'They play my kind of football and I believe the move will give me a platform to break into the England setup. I can be the next Glenn Hoddle. I supported Tottenham as a boy and Glenn was my idol. I have every confidence I can do a similar job for the club.'

I took a bit of flak over that from Ipswich fans. People, quite rightly, didn't like it. That's not what I said, though. Those who knew me, knew that.

Tottenham had just controversially parted ways with manager Terry Venables after an eighth-place finish, a personality clash with Alan Sugar having been widely reported. Ardiles, a former fans' favourite at White Hart Lane, was brought in to win back hearts and minds.

After making me his first signing, Ossie said, 'We have some great young talent at the club, but we are short on experience and in Jason we have signed quality.'

All in all, the pressure was on. You have to remember, I was still only 25. Tottenham fans and the media mocked my 'bold' Hoddle comments. The way that was spun made me look arrogant when that wasn't the case. I wasn't fit to lace Hoddle's boots – I knew that. When I came up against him as a teenager he gave me the complete runaround. He'd do this move, a shoulder shimmy, then go the other way and beat me every time. He could dribble and pass with both feet, nutmeg you, do all sorts. I did not enjoy that experience. I was supposed to do that to people and I didn't like it happening to me. I had nightmares about that for weeks. I'd wake up in the middle of the night in a cold sweat shouting 'Hoddle!'

Starting life at Tottenham with that comparison hanging over me was certainly not helpful. I needed to find my feet in new surroundings, but instead people were expecting me to tear it up from the off.

I spent the first few months living in a hotel. I'd just tied the knot with my childhood girlfriend Leonie in the June, but married life started with us living apart. Missing home, I regularly had several mates come down from Ipswich to visit and we'd rack up huge bar bills. Ossie would call me over in training on Monday. 'Jason, what's this bill for 15 hundred pounds all about?' 'Sorry Ossie, it won't happen again.' But it did. Repeatedly. Ossie, who was such a nice, positive man, would always look at me all disappointed. 'Jason, it's two and a half thousand this time.' 'Sorry Ossie, I promise that's the last time!' That went on and on. It only ever resulted in a little slap on the wrist.

Nowadays when a club buys a player they leave no stone unturned. They dig deep into his social media, get lots of references and find out exactly what sort of character he is. I'm not sure Tottenham did their background checks on me, though. Ossie bought me on my ability alone. He probably just remembered coming up against me as a young player and how I'd done against his struggling Newcastle team during Ipswich's promotion season.

I made some good friends. Gary Mabbutt was a great guy and a great captain. Justin Edinburgh, rest in peace, was a good pal. I got on with Colin Calderwood and David Kerslake, who both signed for the club that summer. But it never felt like that close-knit community we'd had at Ipswich. Everyone was so spread out – people lived in Hertfordshire, the other side of London, all over the place. After training people would head in different directions rather than coming together in one place to bond.

I wasn't settled at all. I was coming back home all the time and meeting up with my former team-mates in Ipswich. One such night led to an incident which I'm not particularly proud of.

I'd met Chris Kiwomya in town for some drinks. I was at the bar on my own and this one guy kept making digs about me going to Tottenham. He just would not leave me alone. In the end I thought, 'I've had enough of this.' I don't know why, but someone had left a pavlova on the bar. I picked it up. *Bang!* Right in his face. There was cake everywhere.

The drama didn't end there. You used to be able to drive through to the Buttermarket in those days and I'd parked right outside that bar. That's how blasé I was. Someone must have rang the police because as I came out of the bar there were a couple of officers standing in the doorway waiting for me. I clocked them, left the car there, went and got something to eat at my mum's house, then came back about three hours later thinking I was clever. I got in the car, turned on the engine and they came running out of the darkness of a shop doorway to nick me. What an idiot. I've had some nutty days and that one was right up there.

The police are funny. Every time I've been done there's always one that will ask for an autograph. Always. Whether they are taking the piss or not I don't know. But you always get one.

I lived in Broughton Road at that time, only a mile or so out of town. Why didn't I walk home? Why not just get a taxi? I know that's what people will say. They're right to do so. I get that now. But, as I'll come on to in the next chapter, there was a disconnect in my mind at that time. I felt a growing sense of entitlement. I've just got to acknowledge that. *I wish it didn't happen, but it did.*

Despite all this off-field drama, my Tottenham career got off to a decent start on the pitch. We went to Newcastle on the opening day. They'd just come up, the place was buoyant, but I almost scored and we won 1-0. I absolutely loved it. I was thinking, 'This is great, this is what I came for.'

Our next game was Arsenal at home. I'm an Ipswich boy, so for me no other derby was going to live up to Norwich in terms of my emotions, but I was well aware of what it meant. Driving up to the stadium you could feel it in the air. The north London derby has proper hate. I was up against Martin Keown that day. Sometimes they would put him in midfield to stop people playing. He was a little rat and just followed me everywhere. That was a tough game for me because I wasn't used to having the scrutiny of a player of that calibre. He completely marked me out of the game. If I remember right, a draw would have been the right result, but they got a late goal through Ian Wright to win 1-0. I had a header saved late on.

The pain of that defeat was quickly softened by wins against Manchester City and Liverpool. I was involved in the winner at Anfield, forcing a save out of Bruce Grobbelaar with Teddy Sheringham finishing the rebound.

Teddy was the person who surprised me the most when I joined Spurs. I didn't realise how good he was. I'd seen him from afar and thought 'he's OK', but then I became his team-mate and he blew me away. He could read the game, technically was great, two feet, could head, could hold it up, could score goals. He was on fire in those opening months of the 1993/94 season.

Darren Anderton, who'd joined from Portsmouth the previous summer, clearly had something about him too. Him and Teddy had a great relationship. It was telepathic. Then you had a teenage Sol Campbell. He'd just been converted from a big centre-forward to a marauding centre-back. What a player he turned out to be.

My first Spurs goal came courtesy of a scruffy finish in a 2-2 draw at Sheffield United. The following weekend I netted in front of the home fans at White Hart Lane when wrapping up a 5-0 win against Oldham. Up next was a trip to Ipswich.

Let's say I wasn't given the warmest welcome back to Portman Road. With word of 'the cake incident' having quickly worked its way around town, I ran on to the pitch to chants of, 'Where's your licence gone? Where's your licence gone?!' That was from all four sides of the ground. It wasn't malicious, it was just tongue-in-cheek. I could take that. Another song that started up during the game wasn't so nice, though. 'Chim chiminey, chim chiminey, chim chim cher-roo! Dozzell was a farmer and now he's a Jew.' I was booed throughout.

Teddy's header put us 1-0 up at the break, but Simon Milton levelled it up, Colin Calderwood was shown his marching orders for a second booking and Ian Marshall put Ipswich 2-1 ahead with ten minutes to go. That, it seemed, was that.

But then, with time running out, a long ball forward was flicked on by Teddy and my old pals David Linighan and Craig Forrest got themselves in a right muddle. As Craig came off his line, David stumbled to the floor and poked the ball past his own keeper to present me with an absolute gift. I just had to pass the ball into an unguarded net from six yards out. I couldn't miss.

Emotion took over. I leapt around like a lunatic in front of the North Stand, swinging my arms and making it clear

I'd enjoyed having the last laugh. However, when my team-mates eventually grabbed me to join in the celebrations something happened that floored me. As I stood still, chest puffed out, and looked up at the crowd I could see that there were a lot of Ipswich fans clapping. *They're happy for me.* That really got me. If you watch the footage back on YouTube you can pinpoint the exact moment where the smile falls from my face.

I knew immediately I'd made a mistake. I can't stand in the North Stand for all those years, then score in front of that end and go nuts. I should have just done the old muted celebration, kept my hands down by my side and gestured to my team-mates to let me have a moment. Unfortunately, that wasn't me at that time.

That was just a guy not thinking about the bigger picture. You score a goal, you celebrate. Simple as that. I never think though, that's the problem. I just do and then face the consequences. That is not right. Once again, *I wish it never happened, but it did.* Once again, not my finest hour. I wish that's the last time I have to write that in this book, but sadly it's not.

With my boosted wages burning a hole in my pocket, I went and bought myself a new BMW 328 convertible. I paid four grand for that car, which was a lot of money in '93, and got myself a personalised 'J12' number plate. Then one day I came back out of Hollywoods nightclub to find it had been keyed the whole way around twice. Someone was either not happy about my celebration or just jealous. Either way, I didn't make the mistake of parking it there again.

Teddy Sheringham had started that season on fire, scoring nine in ten, but a nasty Bryan Robson tackle from behind saw him hobble off in a 2-1 defeat at Manchester United. Gordon Durie fell out with Ossie and left for Rangers. Then John Fashanu left Gary Mabbutt with a fractured skull and eye socket at Wimbledon. That's the worst challenge I've seen on a football pitch. It was a vicious elbow. Gary's face just caved in. We all went to the hospital after the game to see him. He was an absolute mess. I've still got a picture in my head now of what he looked like. Gary's one of the nicest guys in football and he didn't deserve that.

Personally, I had a good little spell. I flicked the ball on for Darren Anderton's opener against Arsenal at Highbury, but Ian Wright equalised in the second half to make it nine league games without a win. I scored both our goals in a 2-0 victory at Manchester City the following week. I provided another headed assist, for Vinny Samways this time, in a thrilling 3-3 home draw with Liverpool. I then contributed a goal and assist in a 3-1 comeback win at West Ham just after Christmas. That was three goals and three assists in five games.

We really hit the rocks in January, though. Aston Villa ended our League Cup run. It needed a replay and penalty shoot-out to scrape through an FA Cup third round tie against second-tier strugglers Peterborough. We then lost 2-1 at lowly Swindon in the league.

I watched the FA Cup fourth round draw just knowing what was coming. Ipswich Town versus … Tottenham Hotspur. 'Told you!' I said to the lads, with a smile, the next day. These things always seem to happen. They do to me, anyway.

I went into that game thinking about how I would react far more respectfully if I scored at Portman Road again. I need not have worried about that. We got done 3-0 with a couple of goals coming at corners. This time, all the drama for me happened off the field.

That match proved to be the start of a lengthy feud between my brother Tony and the Spurs fans. He didn't go looking for trouble with the supporters of my new club that January afternoon, but let's just say he didn't walk away from it either. It was a scene that, as I outlined earlier, was commonplace back then. Tony was in the Pioneer Stand watching the game from behind the dugouts when suddenly around 20 undercover Tottenham fans made themselves known in that area. Bad idea. They came off second best.

After the game I went for a drink in town with Tony and the lads at the Earl Roberts pub. They were just filling me in on their scrap when those same Tottenham boys who had taken a bit of a beating came bursting through the door looking for revenge. God knows how they'd tracked us down.

You could cut the atmosphere with a knife as the two groups faced off. It was like something from a western. I quickly stepped in to act as mediator. 'Sorry about the result and what's happened, but please don't do this because it's just going to be chaos.' Bearing in mind they weren't very happy with me either, given the way I'd played that day, that appeal initially got short shrift. But I persevered. 'Look, I can see where you're coming from lads, I really can, but this can't happen. This is not the way.' It took some serious persuading on my part to defuse the situation and for them to walk away.

Two months later, with Tottenham now very much dragged into a relegation fight, Ipswich came to White Hart Lane for the return league fixture. Chris Kiwomya gave Ipswich the lead, but it was my headed knock-down that set up Nick Barmby's equaliser. It finished 1-1.

Tony had gone down there for the game with my mum and some other people who had been nothing to do with the first incident. He thought that would all be forgotten about. Wrong. Those Spurs fans had been waiting for their moment to have the final say. They'd done their homework, knew exactly where in the ground I'd get Tony tickets and had eyeballs on him the whole match. They never let him out of their sight.

After the game, one of Tony's mates went and got the car and pulled up outside the main gates to pick up him and my mum. They all got in, ready to head home, when about 100 Tottenham fans were given the signal and came running out of their main pub on Tottenham High Road just 50 yards away.

This was a fight even Tony couldn't win and he knew it. He jumped out the car and turned into prime Colin Jackson, hurdling fence after fence to get away. He was frantically knocking on people's doors to let him in along the way and eventually found refuge. I genuinely think he would have been a dead man had he not done that.

Tony's two mates had also scattered. The Tottenham fans, having lost their main targets, then turned back on the car and, with my mum still in it on her own, they smashed the windows in with bricks. She was terrified, obviously. Still, she was the only one who didn't run. I joked with Tony afterwards, 'You haven't got the title of "hardest in the family" any more!'

I guess Tony was naive, but I can't be mad at him because I didn't know those sort of people operated like that. He should have been more aware of the potential danger and not put Mum in harm's way. Like me though, he just didn't think. With the benefit of hindsight, he was always going to be a target that day. If you come to Ipswich and take a bit of a hiding, they are not letting that go. People don't forget. They'll wait until the return fixture – and that's what happened.

It circulated around the fanbase what had occurred. On the pitch I'd go for a throw-in and hear Tottenham fans calling out, 'Oi, Dozzell, where's your fucking brother?' I'd be out for the Christmas party with the lads, having a good time, then that familiar question came my way. 'Where's your brother? He's dead.' I'd plead with them, 'Come on mate, give me a break, will you?' That carried on for the whole four years I was at the club. They never forgot. My team-mates were bemused by the whole scenario. Stuff like that doesn't happen to normal people.

Teddy Sheringham returned to give the team a timely lift in April. A 3-0 home win against Southampton was huge. A 2-0 win at Oldham secured us safety with a game to spare.

I'd finished my debut season at Spurs with 11 goals and a few assists, but events on and off the field meant I wasn't exactly leading any popularity contests with fans of my old club or new.

14

Trial and Error

AS MY career took off, my personality started to change.

Two things I didn't have much of as a child came into play – money and adoration. Mum had shown me plenty of love of course, but my circle was small. What I got from football fans was widespread attention. I won't lie, I found that intoxicating.

I shouldn't have needed that. I should have been getting my personality and confidence from family and friends, from the people who didn't just know me as a footballer, from the people who could truly tap into me.

Instead, fame created an ego and money fuelled it. Those things collided. That wasn't going to work. Not for me. I'd developed no social skills up to the age of 16, I hadn't got anyone there guiding me, so I was going into everything blind. It was all trial and error. That's been the story of my life.

It was just a case of 'he's got a talent, away you go' and hope for the best. My safest place was on the pitch. Beyond that I didn't have the tools to know what was going on properly. Not 100 per cent.

When I was at Ipswich and we played the likes of Tottenham, Arsenal or Chelsea, their players would keep saying to us in the players' lounge afterwards, 'Come out in London.' They told me about a place called The Spot in Covent Garden where all the footballers congregated. Chris Kiwomya and I went and hung out with the likes of Ian Wright and Les Ferdinand. It was great. I was going down most weeks after that.

Sometimes Leonie would come with me to London, sometimes not. We liked the music scene and we used to meet friends. Legends, Ministry of Sound, Emporium, the Gas Club – London nights out in the '90s were just magical.

I spent loads on a BMW, Gucci clothes and Rolex watches. I was bloody useless with money. I just liked nice things. I talk to my son Andre now and he gets so much financial advice from his agency. I was just chucked some money and expected to get on with it.

In October '92, after I'd scored to seal a 4-2 home win against Leeds on Ipswich's way to promotion, I went to Stringfellows with a mate. I looked across the room and saw boxer Nigel Benn, who at that time was preparing for a world super-middleweight title fight. He looked at me, I looked at him and he mimed my stooping header from earlier in the day as if to say, 'Yeah, I saw your goal.'

We got talking and ended up becoming good friends. I went to most of his fights, all the Chris Eubank ones, and some after-parties at his house too.

Every time we went out, he'd say 'I've got your back' which was good to know!

Increasingly, I lived for the moment. I was susceptible to anything. I'd do something and then face the consequences after. I never had that voice that says 'this isn't the right thing to do'. That's always been me.

I've always been one of those characters who will try anything once. Is that because I transitioned from not a lot to a hell of lot almost overnight? Is it because I was surrounded by people who were encouraging me to push my boundaries? Some people can say 'no'. Some people can walk away. I have never been one of those people. 'You coming out?' 'Yeah, all right.' Always.

You become surrounded by false people who you think are good friends. That's not reality. You get sucked in. You should be keeping those people at arm's length and maintaining a close network of people you can trust and listen to. Don't be rude to these people, say hello, but keep them at a distance. You don't need many in that trusted network, only two or three. Just listen to them. I know that now, but I didn't know that then. Back then I took everybody in. And I mean everybody. All different kinds of people.

I met Leonie when I was 15 and we married when I was 25, the year I signed for Tottenham. We'd had a few issues before that, all my fault, but things were meant to be looking up for us that summer.

Dion, my eldest son, was born in 1995. I could be a brilliant husband and father Monday to Friday, but that all went out the window come Saturday night. The problem was there were just no boundaries when I left the house.

I wasn't prolific in my career, but I loved scoring goals. I used to like waking up Sunday morning, getting the papers and seeing 'Dozzell 58' or whatever. It was the best feeling. That created a problem for me because whenever it happened I would have to go out to celebrate. If I'd scored and we'd won, I'd tell my wife 'see you Sunday afternoon'. When that final whistle sounded I came into the dressing room knowing exactly what I was going to do. I had a plan. That's what London can do to you.

Did I enjoy the lifestyle more than the football? All I can say is that if I could get both together that was great. I did feel it if we lost, don't get me wrong. I always have done. But if we won, I knew my night was going to get really, really good. If we won, I would be celebrating.

There was a lot of attention from the opposite sex. I didn't really have to do anything. It was crazy. I turned into as good a womaniser as I was a footballer. Usually it was just talking, flirting, dancing – sometimes it went further – but it never meant anything. Whatever I'd done, the feelings would be gone the next morning. I wouldn't feel much at all.

I wouldn't have left my wife for anyone. It wasn't like that. The next day I would just think 'OK, that happened' and move on. My moral compass was off. I didn't have the tools to think rationally. There was no thinking at all most of the time.

Did my wife know what was going on? Of course she did. She had to. I assume she just turned a blind eye to it. I was providing us with a nice lifestyle. She'd give me a rollicking and the cycle would continue. We'd argue, we'd split, then one of us would say 'I still love you, come back'. It was on-off all the time. We had that kind of relationship.

I definitely got selfish and lost track of who was important to me in the search for cheap thrills. I lost touch with my real friends. I became distant from my best mate Pasquale, who I'd known since I was seven. We got it back when I finished football. I had to tell him, 'Sorry, I just lost myself.'

There was a period of disconnect in my brain about what was right and wrong. I became very selfish. I always did what Jason Dozzell wanted to do. I thought I was entitled for some reason. That's not right.

London was a whole different ball game to Ipswich. In those first few months at Tottenham, I didn't socialise that much. As I said before, it didn't have that same sort of close-knit feel of Ipswich. I soon got into it, though, and once I'd been there about a year I was gripped by life in the capital.

I soon realised I was living in the biggest playground in the world. There was something to do every night of the week. Monday, Tuesday, Wednesday, Thursday, Friday – there was always temptation. Some places didn't open until 6am.

On one of my first nights out as a Tottenham player, it may even have been the very first, a random guy came up to me, shook my hand, said 'have a good night' and walked off. I looked down and he'd slipped a bag of cocaine into my hand. I went and chucked it straight down the toilet. Drugs scared the shit out of me.

I wondered whether it was a trick or a setup, but soon realised that was just London life. Everyone was doing it. I saw players from all different clubs regularly ducking off to the toilets. It was obvious what they were up to. I think football fans would be shocked to hear some of the names involved.

Being the try-anything-once character I am, it didn't take much encouragement for me to eventually give it a go. The first time I did cocaine I felt like Superman. It's not a good drug, though. Millions of people do it socially, but if it grabs you the wrong way you are screwed. It's just a fake feeling. I found that later in life.

I can't sit here and say that was a dark time for me, though. Not at all. London in the '90s had such a magical vibe. Everyone was happy, or so it seemed. I can't say that I didn't enjoy that period.

On nights out you'd see all the celebrities – singers, soap stars, the lot. I was in a nightclub one night and this girl kept tapping me on the shoulder. For some reason I didn't turn around on that particular occasion. I don't know why. I guess that night I just couldn't be bothered. Off she went and my mate, who couldn't believe what he'd just witnessed, goes to me, 'You know who that was, don't you?!' 'No?' 'That was Baby Spice!'

When the summer arrived, I took things to extremes. That three-month period off was when I would go against the grain. I would do an ecstasy tablet here and there – once every couple of weeks, just to fit in. I'd never do it during the season because there was drug testing, but during the summer I'd have a little blast. I'd go to Ibiza and just go nuts. It made me feel good. I didn't feel bad because everybody else was doing it.

That became the pattern. Just wait for the season to finish and let my hair down. I'd behave like a lunatic, really go for it, and then two weeks before the start of the new campaign get stuck into pre-season training. I wasn't alone. Loads of players would come back completely out of shape. In our minds, that's what pre-season was for – to get rid of the beer belly.

I wasn't thinking straight about where I wanted to go in my career. The focus had gone. *I wish it never happened, but it did happen*. I have to accept that. I can't tip-toe around it. I have to tell the truth, get this out and move forward with my life.

I don't care who you are, if you were in my shoes – life skills at a low ebb, young and psychologically not ready – I bet you wouldn't have handled it either. People like to point fingers, but it's not as simple as that.

I was never pulled in the right direction. That was hard for me. I needed more substance from somebody who was going to truly look after me. But I was pretty much left alone.

I love my mum to bits, but being that young man out there in the world – that's when a father figure comes into play. I speak to Andre before and after every game he plays. 'How are you?' 'Are you feeling any pressure?' 'How did you sleep last night?' 'What are you doing tonight?' I would have loved that just once. There was no Friday pep talk or Saturday debrief for me.

You need to speak to someone who properly knows you. If you don't, you end up dealing with everything yourself and that can get you polluted over a period of time. You're not processing anything or learning. That's why my trial-and-error cycle repeated all through my adult life.

Instead, I was surrounded by people who didn't have my best interests at heart. I wouldn't call them hangers-on, they just went along with all the fun when what I needed was someone to say, 'What the hell are you doing?' I realise now that a good friend is someone telling you something that you don't want to hear. I didn't have one person to say, 'Calm down, you don't have to go mad all the time.'

I was naive and followed the crowd, but that doesn't make it right. I let myself and other people down. I know that now. I should never have touched cocaine because that affected me later in life in a different way.

There were always going to be consequences at some point. You don't get immunity. Things will always come back and bite you on the arse at some stage.

I lost focus. I stopped doing what had got me to the Premier League. A football career that could have taken off, unsurprisingly, very quickly stagnated.

15

Terror Tuesdays

LET'S GO back to the summer of 1994. While Wet, Wet, Wet's 'Love Is All Around' stayed at the top of the UK charts for a record 15 successive weeks, things were in a constant state of flux at White Hart Lane.

In July, as punishment for financial irregularities committed under the previous owners during the 1980s, Spurs were hit with the heaviest punishment ever handed out by the Football Association. The club was docked 12 points ahead of the forthcoming campaign, banned from the FA Cup for a season and fined £600,000.

We'd just finished four points above the drop and, to make matters worse, the 1994/95 campaign was going to see four teams, rather than three, relegated in order to streamline the division from 22 to 20 clubs. In short, it wasn't looking good.

Personally, I had some bad breaks too – quite literally. During one early pre-season training session I landed awkwardly and fractured my left wrist. That, unfortunately, is not where this tale ends.

A few days later I went out in Ipswich. I was making my way through the Wine Bar alone, my mates had gone on ahead, and this guy made a comment. I should have just kept walking, learning my lesson from pavlova-gate, but I turned and snapped, 'What the fuck did you say?'

Before I knew it – boom! – he'd head-butted me right on the nose. I was in shock. I staggered off, got to the end of the bar and blood started gushing out my nose. My mates saw the state of me, I told them what had happened and suddenly there was a huge commotion. They went and found this guy, dragged him outside and – this next bit is something I'm not proud of – I punched him in the back of the head. I just had this moment where I completely lost it.

I should say here that for the most part everyone was great with me in Ipswich, but for every 20 people who are nice you always get one who's going to try it on. I should have been better at not reacting.

I woke up the next morning in pain. Turns out I'd broken the other wrist. Tottenham phoned me up. 'We've heard there was a fight.' 'No, no, no. I just fell on it.' Somehow, I got away with that excuse.

While I was healing, a defiant Alan Sugar funded a shopping spree. In August, just days before the new season kicked off, three eye-catching deals were completed. German star Jürgen Klinsmann and the Romanian duo Ilie Dumitrescu and Gheorghe Popescu were signed for a combined £7.5m from Monaco, Steaua Bucharest and PSV Eindhoven respectively.

It was a much-needed boost for the club, but less so for me. With an embarrassment of forward riches, Ossie adopted an all-out attacking philosophy. Klinsmann, Sheringham, Anderton, Barmby and Dumitrescu were soon dubbed 'The Famous Five'. With my two broken wrists, I had to watch on enviously.

I was actually the first player to meet Jürgen. I was in hospital when he arrived to have his medical. He knew my name, which surprised me. I was made up by that. Jürgen used to turn up to training in his Volkswagen Beetle – the media loved that. He probably had ten Ferraris in his garage at home, but it helped soften the public mood over a player who had broken English hearts – including mine – at Italia '90. Then he did that famous 'dive' celebration in an opening-day 4-3 win at Sheffield Wednesday, a tongue-in-cheek response to the cheat accusations, and the league had a new star. I had a lot of time for Jürgen. What a player and what a guy.

Even though I wasn't playing, that was still a fun time. Training was brilliant with Ossie because it was just five-a-sides every day – and I was a brilliant five-a-side player. There wasn't much work on tactics or discussions about high press, low press and all of that. It was just 'go out and play'.

Bones finally healed, I returned to the team in early October. When we clicked in attack, we were unstoppable. But we started getting picked off after a while. People saw how open we were and exploited it.

Following a 5-2 defeat at Manchester City we went to Notts County in the League Cup. They were a team that would go on to finish bottom of the First Division that season, but we went 2-0 down early on, Dumitrescu was sent off for a second yellow before half-time and we lost 3-0. Off the back of that, Ossie was sacked.

Just like with Bobby Ferguson, I felt bad. I was Ossie's first signing and now he was gone. Had I done enough for him? You always ask yourself that. There's no doubt change was needed, though. There were no defensive units anywhere. Five up front, one in midfield and four at the back. It was disjointed. It felt like we had to score five goals to win a game. There was no Plan B.

Steve Perryman had a couple of games as caretaker manager. The first was a 3-1 home win against West Ham, the second was at big-spending Blackburn (who, with Alan Shearer and Chris Sutton up top, would go on to win the title).

Everything went wrong for me that day at Ewood Park. Nothing, and I mean nothing, came off. I'm talking the basics. It's like the golfer when he hits one in the water, hits another one in the water and then their head's gone. I just couldn't seem to do anything right.

Eventually I was dragged off after 29 minutes. It wasn't a nice feeling when the board went up, I can tell you. I protested – 'You could have waited until half-time!' – but I knew it was the right decision. All players have one or two of those games in their careers; they're lying if they say otherwise. Unfortunately, it happened to me on a day when we were all auditioning ahead of a new manager being appointed.

It's weird. Sometimes you wake up and you just know if you're going to have a good or a bad game. You can just feel it. Every time I had a good game, I knew it was going to happen because I woke up feeling energised and that built up. Sometimes though, if you've eaten the wrong things, if you haven't got enough sleep, if you've got other things going on in your life and on your mind, you just feel flat. Then it becomes mental.

I still had my moan when I went to see the manager on the Monday. You have to do that to show you've got something about you. We went over a few things and I said, 'Look, I hold my hands up, I didn't play well, but I'm letting you know I'm not happy.' I think the manager would want you to do that rather than not come in at all. If you say nothing that makes it look like you've just accepted it. That's how I'd see it anyway if I was the manager. I would want the player to come and see me rather than just leave it.

After that, Gerry Francis was appointed. Him and Ossie were chalk and cheese in terms of how they operated. It was a completely different mindset and philosophy, both for training and how we played. It was more disciplined. A rigid 4-4-2. He changed everything straight away.

At that time, my favourite night of the week was 'Ladies' Night' on a Monday at Stringfellows. Then Gerry came along and introduced something called 'Terror Tuesdays'. He'd make us run and run and run. A box-to-box sprint, 30 seconds' rest, a double box-to-box sprint, 30 seconds' rest, a double box-to-box sprint and then back to the halfway line. There'd be about 40 of these sprints in total.

I used to come in on a couple of hours' sleep and do all that. God almighty, it was tough. I always made it in though, no matter what. It never crossed my mind to ring in and cry off. That wouldn't be good for me mentally. Those Tuesday sessions really were horrific. It was probably what we needed in fairness though because I don't think we were fit enough under Ossie.

Results picked up. In December, the 12-point deduction and FA Cup ban was revoked after a successful appeal. Jürgen kept scoring, we climbed the table, went on a run to the FA Cup semi-final before losing to eventual winners Everton and ultimately finished seventh. I wasn't involved in any of that, though. After getting hooked at Blackburn, it was more than six months before I featured for the first team again. Gerry eventually handed me a late cameo on the final day of the season against Leeds.

To be honest, I wasn't as frustrated as I should have been. My focus had slipped. I was going out more and more. I was, as previously outlined, enjoying London life.

I still trained with the first team, but the only time I played was in the odd reserve game once a month or so to keep ticking over. And when I was playing reserve football I took less care over when I went out and how I went out. The disappointment of not being in the first-team squad on a Saturday was offset by the fact I could now go out on a Friday night. OK, there'd be a bit of training on a Saturday morning, but I could get through that. Then I'd do Saturday night as usual, follow it up with a Sunday night at either Charlie Chans in Walthamstow or Epping Forest Country Club, then a Monday night at Stringfellows in the city. I always did just enough in those midweek reserve games. Get it, give it. After a while you just get used to that being the norm.

Another turbulent summer at Spurs rolled around. Klinsmann, Popescu and Barmby were all sold. A team full of youngsters and reserves (not including me) then lost 8-0 to FC Cologne in the much-maligned Intertoto Cup.

Chris Armstrong was signed as Klinsmann's replacement in a £4.5m deal from Crystal Palace. There were chants of 'what a waste of money' aimed at him, which I thought was unfair and unhelpful. My professional opinion is that Chris was a good player and he answered those critics with a decent number of goals that season.

It was certainly a negative arena at Tottenham in the '90s. I soon realised that Ipswich is nothing like a big London club when the fans get on your back. The expectations were just so much higher and they will let you know if you're not meeting them.

There were only a few who got left alone – mainly the England boys, Teddy, Darren Anderton, Gary Mabbutt, Sol Campbell – but the rest of us were only as good as our last pass. If you gave the ball away the crowd would turn on you. It could be very, very harsh. Most of us would get it at some stage, but the regulars would be me, Vinny Samways, Chris Armstrong, plus Ruel Fox now and again.

Hearing the whole crowd groan when you give the ball away is the worst thing. Often there'd be fans waiting by the players' exit after the game to let off some steam. You'd have to scramble to get in your car and get away down Tottenham High Road. I've seen players be sick before a game at White Hart Lane because of the fear factor. Overcoming that is a real mental challenge.

I'm not getting my violin out here, by the way. Criticism is part of the game. I accept that. Fans who pay their hard-earned money are entitled to an opinion. I never forgot what it was like to be a supporter myself. I'd feel bad when that criticism came my way, but it never stopped me doing what I had to do. I saw it as a challenge. What have you got? Are you going to shy away or stand up?

As I said earlier, another thing I found very different being at a London club was that there wasn't that community feel that I had at Ipswich. Players didn't socialise together as one. It was very cliquey and not in a good way. We had our little group – me, Sol Campbell, who became godfather to my oldest boy, Chris Armstrong, Foxy and Steve Slade, who was a young kid. All black boys. I get on with everyone, I'm not like that, but that's the way the groups ended up forming for some reason.

Having not enjoyed living in a hotel during the early part of my Tottenham career, I came back to Ipswich and commuted every day. I'd meet Justin Edinburgh at Brentwood and we'd take it in turns to drive in. I had a spell living at Waltham Abbey, but it wasn't long before I was back in Ipswich again.

It was great when we signed Ruel Fox. Foxy was a fellow Ipswich boy who was born less than a month after me. I didn't see him much growing up, but I'd heard about him. He ended up starting out at Norwich, but I got past that as we became really good friends. He was some player. Ipswich missed a trick with him.

For a while, when I was banned from the road, Foxy drove us in. Then he lost his licence too, so we had to get a driver. We had to employ our mate, a guy called Dodi, to take us in each day.

The party continued after a final day 3-1 home win against Brighton clinched the First Division title.
Newsquest

The promotion-winning squad of 1991/92. We were so bonded as a group on and off the pitch. Back row (l-r): Craig Forrest, Gavin Johnson, Steve Whitton, Eddie Youds, Neil Thompson, Phil Whelan, Romeo Zondervan, Steve Palmer, Frank Yallop, Glenn Pennyfather, John Wark and David Gregory. Front: Mick Stockwell, Paul Goddard, Chris Kiwomya, David Linighan, me and Simon Milton.
Newsquest

Celebrating winning the title alongside Simon Milton, Chris Kiwomya and John Wark. I never tire of seeing this picture on the outside of the Cobbold Stand. Newsquest

John Lyall holds the First Division title, flanked by Chris Kiwomya, David Linighan, myself and Romeo Zondervan. We didn't have the best team that season, but we had the best manager. Getty

Following relegation in 1986, I'd vowed to get Ipswich Town back in the big time. Winning the First Division title was the proudest moment of my career.
Alamy

Scoring the first of my two goals in a crucial East Anglian derby win at Portman Road in April '93. I'd been brought up to hate Norwich City and had a good record against them in my career.
Newsquest

Up against Liverpool's Paul Stewart during a 0-0 draw at Anfield in February 1994. After a flying start to life back in the Premier League, teams started to work us out.
Newsquest

Pictured the summer I signed for Spurs. I was under pressure to deliver from the off following my mis-quoted Glenn Hoddle comments.
Alamy

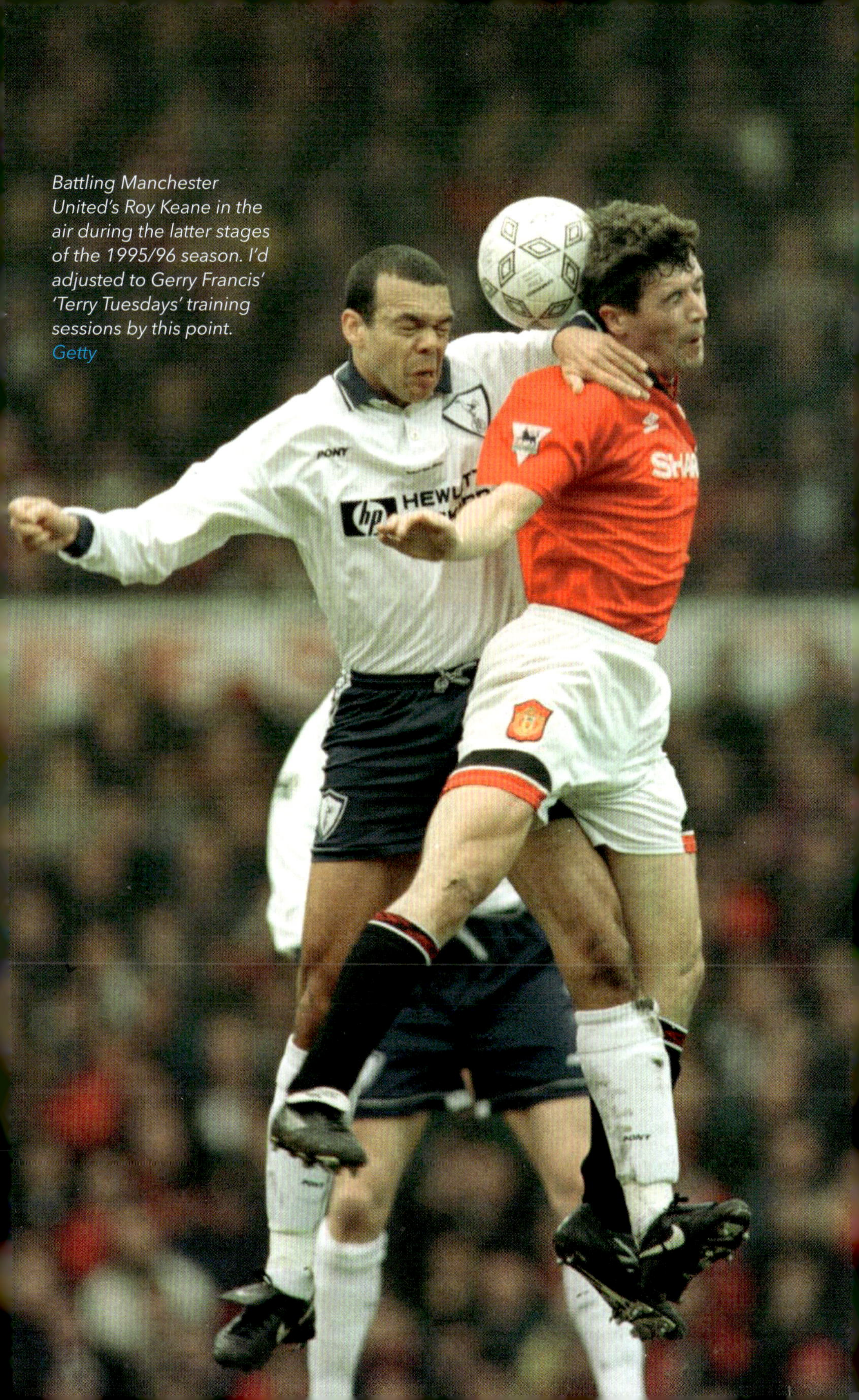

Battling Manchester United's Roy Keane in the air during the latter stages of the 1995/96 season. I'd adjusted to Gerry Francis' 'Terry Tuesdays' training sessions by this point. Getty

Celebrating a well-taken goal at Newcastle on the final day of the 95/96 season. Tottenham were on course for European football at that stage.
Colorsport

My second spell at Ipswich started so well. Here I am celebrating after sealing a 2-0 home win against Bury in October '97.
Newsquest

I loved my time as Ipswich Wanderers manager. Being associated with a team in the town again renewed my spirits. Newsquest

Outside Ipswich Magistrates' Court following my drink driving conviction in 2008. Frustrated with life, I was on a slow descent to a dark place. Newsquest

With my son Andre not long after he'd turned 14. There was a buzz surrounding his progress from quite early on. Newsquest

Andre comes on for his Town debut, at Hillsborough, in April 2016. Watching from the stands, it was like I was transported back to 1984. Pagepix Ltd/Newsquest

Go on my son! Andre heads home on his debut against Sheffield Wednesday aged 16. He wasn't quite as young as when I did it though!
Pagepix Ltd/Newsquest

A point in my direction after history had repeated. The tears were flowing. It must have been fate.
Pagepix Ltd/Newsquest

Helping Ipswich Town reach the semi-finals of the FA Youth Cup was the highlight of my time coaching in the club's academy. Here I am consoling Albie Armin after defeat to Liverpool – I played with his dad at Langham Lions! Newsquest

With Darren Anderton suffering a long-term injury, I had a lot more game time in that third season with Spurs. The style of play became a bit more direct. We still played some football, but we'd get the ball forward a bit quicker with Chris Armstrong running in behind.

I intercepted the ball in the build-up to Chris's winner against Arsenal at White Hart Lane. Ian Walker kept five clean sheets in a row after that. Come December we were third in the table. It felt like things were getting back on track.

A muscle strain kept me out for the festive period. I promise you that was genuine. I may have liked going out, but I never went missing over Christmas. I really enjoyed playing at that time of year. I was certainly gutted to miss a 4-1 win against champions elect Manchester United on New Year's Day.

The only injury I'd had at Ipswich was a broken ankle. I'd never had niggles before, but now I was starting to get a few – little things that would keep me out for two or three weeks at a time. Was it the drive in from Ipswich each day? Was London life starting to kick in? It was a combination of those things, I think. My priorities certainly weren't right. I thought I could get away with it because everyone else was doing the same thing.

Arsène Wenger started to change all that, didn't he? I remember Chris Kiwomya telling me that alcohol had been banned from the players' lounge at Arsenal. That blew our minds. Would things have been different for me had I ended up at a club like that? No. I don't think so. I think wherever I would have gone it would still have been the same, unfortunately.

On the final day of that season we went to Newcastle. Following Kevin Keegan's 'I would love it' rant, they needed to win and hope Manchester United lost to claim the title. We needed to win to qualify for Europe. The stakes were high. We went 1-0 up with a great goal from me. Outside the box, little Cruyff turn and I whipped one in. I was pleased with that. They equalised late on though, it finished 1-1 and neither of us accomplished what we wanted to.

The squad flew out to Marbella straight after that for a jolly-up and then attentions turned to Euro '96. As I said before, I was a massive England fan and I watched that run to the semis on home soil thinking, 'This is it, football's coming home.' My old under-21s team-mate Gazza was just a millimetre away from getting his toe on that ball against Germany in extra time, but it wasn't to be.

Straight after that tournament, Tony Adams got pissed and crashed his car. He was struggling with mental health at that time and said his mission was to go on the biggest bender he'd ever had. Pressure does things to you. It can make you do stupid things. I can relate to that. You just don't know what's going on in someone's head, do you? Tony, thankfully, tackled his addictions. When you're staring the abyss in the face you have to react.

That summer I got a call out of the blue from someone at Norwich City. 'Hi Jason, we want you, we think there's a deal to be done, are you interested?' I was very quick to reply with a polite, 'Thanks, but no thanks.' I would rather have been broke and sleeping outside Crown Pools than play for them. Look, I respect Norwich as a football club, but I'd been brought up to hate them, so that was a complete non-starter.

What was I thinking as I went into the final year of my four-year contract at Tottenham? I probably wasn't thinking much at all if I'm honest. It was just living for the moment.

In November, I got subbed at half-time of a 6-1 defeat at Bolton in the League Cup. I was having quite a good game to be honest, but the goals were flying in, Gerry had to sacrifice someone and I was the easy one to take out because I hadn't been playing much. In late December, I came on at half-time at Newcastle but had to come off nine minutes later with a calf problem. We lost that game 7-1. That summed up how things were going for me.

I'm proud to say that I always got back in the team at some stage. It was always a case of not being too self-critical and trying to fight through the hard times. That's football. That's what I tell Andre. If you define who you are when you get knocked down, how are you going to get back up?

My time at Tottenham ultimately ended in the summer of 1997 (more on that in the next chapter). I'd scored 14 goals in 93 appearances. How do Spurs fans look back on my time there? Well, I've seen one article online that has me in the club's all-time worst XI. That's just one person's opinion. It is what it is. I shouldn't be in Tottenham's worst ever XI, though. Nowhere near. Who knows, maybe that piece was written by one of the guys who chased Tony down the street?!

I did have some great games for Tottenham, just nowhere near enough of them. It's as simple as that. There are some mitigating factors, while some of the issues were self-inflicted. I got sucked into London life and my focus slipped. What happened between my brother and the fans, plus the general negative vibes around the club didn't help either.

At the end of the day, Tottenham Hotspur is a great football club and I played nearly 100 games for them. Over four years there weren't many long periods where I was completely discarded to the sidelines and that has to say something. That's the way I look at it, anyway.

16

Homecoming and Heartbreak

BELIEVE IT or not, despite the lack of playing time in 1996/97, Tottenham actually wanted to keep me on beyond the end of my four-year deal. One day in training, Gerry Francis quietly came over and said, 'Travel with me to the airport tomorrow.' Then on the way there in his car he said he was going to offer me a new contract. I was delighted. I loved London life.

Everything changed in March though when, again, I was my own worst enemy.

The *Sunday Sport* was running some Girl of the Year competition. I think Ruel Fox had a column in the paper, so he got an invite, and I didn't need much persuading to accompany him. When we got there, David Sullivan, who owned the newspaper, asked me, 'Do you want to be a judge?' Talk about a silly question!

Before the competition started, I used my new role as an excuse to go backstage and introduce myself to all of the girls. One of them took a shine to me. Abusing my position of power, I said, 'I'll put you in the top three if you come and have a drink with me afterwards.' I think I put her second in the end. She didn't deserve second, but I wanted to make her feel good. It worked. We ended up getting a taxi all the way to Oxford, where she lived, and things happened. That was wrong. I was a married man. I hold my hands up. Guilty as charged.

A few days later we played Sunderland away. The night before the game, at the team hotel, I got a knock on my door. It was her. She'd travelled up, asked for my room number at reception and found me without warning. The trouble was, I was rooming with a team-mate – Vinny Samways, if memory serves me correctly – so in hushed tones I told her to go and wait downstairs and quickly shut the door. Then I rang the team doctor and, lying, said, 'I'm ill, I need my own room.' He bought it. I got my own room, she stayed the night and I was absolutely knackered the next day. I didn't make it down for the team breakfast, couldn't raise a gallop in the warm-up and was relieved to remain an unused sub.

'Got away with that,' I thought, in typical fashion. Wrong. A few days later, a call came through on the house phone. My wife took it downstairs in the kitchen while I was upstairs. After a while I thought 'she's been speaking to them for a bit' and went to go and check if everything was OK. 'Get your arse back upstairs!' she snapped. I obliged. Another 20 minutes went by and I went to check again. Same response. I knew I was in trouble, I just didn't know why. Eventually the call ended. It turned out that the *Sunday Sport* girl had called to tell my wife everything. I owned up. Even I couldn't wriggle out of this one.

After that this girl kept ringing me saying she was pregnant. I didn't deal with that at all well. Panicking, I told her in no uncertain terms to have a termination. Bad move. She told me she had taped the calls and the *News of the World* were interested in the story. I panicked. 'Whatever they have offered you, I will double it.' No, she didn't want that. To be honest, I think it was all a set-up.

After a few days of being on tenterhooks about the whole thing, I was out in London one night (surprise, surprise) when someone from the *News of the World* rang me to say, 'The story's going in tomorrow.' I had no chance to properly give my side of things. Apparently, that's what they do. I woke up hungover the next day and trudged to the shop to get a copy. It was a double page spread. The headline was 'Soccer star gets glamour girl pregnant', or something like that.

The same girl had also done a story about Everton striker Duncan Ferguson in the *Sunday Sport* the same day. She claimed to have been with him not long after he'd controversially served time in prison for an on-field head-butt playing for Rangers. This piece was her giving me and Big Dunc marks out of ten. I can't remember the categories, but it was quirky things like 'half-time refreshments' followed by comments like 'Jason brought me water, Duncan champagne – Dozzell 0 Ferguson 9'. This went on and on. I ended up with 16 out of 100. Duncan got 99, or something ridiculous. I played in a golf competition the next day and got nearest to the pin. When I went up for my award afterwards, the trophy had 'Sixteen' written on it instead of my name. Still to this day, friends of mine use the nickname 'Sixteen'. I guess I deserve it.

After all that I got lawyers involved. That girl was made to do a DNA test and it turned out she wasn't even pregnant. I tried to sue the papers, but apparently my case wasn't strong enough. Their legal people said because I had actually been with her she 'could' have been pregnant. The *News of the World* eventually published a two-sentence apology which was buried deep into the paper right where the car adverts were. 'Last week we published a story about Tottenham footballer Jason Dozzell which stated ... blah, blah, blah ... Sorry, we got it wrong.' Footballers were getting trapped left, right and centre by the tabloid press at that time. It was out of control.

That was a really, really hard time. It was horrible for my wife, horrible for my family. Somehow, Leonie didn't leave me after all that. I admitted to everything, we got through it and tried to move on. That said, it was probably a factor in what happened with us much later on.

My wife may have stuck with me, but Tottenham didn't. Gerry Francis obviously thought, 'I don't need this drama, let's just let him go.' I got told there was no longer a contract on the table going into the final game of the season, at home against Coventry. My head was all over the show. I was awful that day. One report of the 2-1 defeat that I've seen online states, 'When Dozzell's late crossfield ball sailed high into the East Stand the supporters' reaction suggested his days at the club were numbered.' So it proved. Having lost my focus, I only had myself to blame.

For the first time in my life I was unemployed. A few foreign clubs showed interest – I actually met representatives from Belgian outfit Standard Liège in London – but that was too much. I was a home boy. I wish I had been equipped for an adventure like that, but I wasn't. Derby, who had just finished mid-table in the Premier League, and Birmingham, who had ambitions of returning to the top flight, also made contact. But they both wanted me to go in on a trial basis and that didn't appeal. I was 29, had just come from Tottenham and, perhaps arrogantly, felt people should know what I could do.

I worked hard that summer. Secretly I was always hoping Ipswich would come in, but I was never going to contact them. My ego prevented that. Then one day I was running the roads near Christchurch Park, trying to get fit, when I bumped into Bryan Klug. He said, 'Come in and see George Burley.' I did and George seemed keen to get something done. It took a little while to agree, though. It wasn't about the money, as reported at the time, rather the length of the contract. They wanted to do until the end of the season, but I wanted two years. Following a bit of a stand-off, the goalposts moved. In the end I cracked and accepted a month-to-month deal. I really should have taken that first offer.

It took me a few reserve games to get up to speed, but before long I was absolutely smashing it. Having always been a midfielder at Tottenham, I returned to a forward role at Ipswich. Playing just off Alex Mathie, I was the man of the match in a 2-0 home win against Manchester United in the League Cup. I had an absolute ball out there that day.

It was at that time an 18-year-old Kieron Dyer was breaking through. I knew of his dad, Charlie, from my brother's circle. Every Sunday in the late '80s, early '90s all the black boys would meet at Christchurch Park following a big night at the Caribbean Club and have these big, free-for-all football matches. Sometimes it would be as many as 20-a-side and, with no referee, it would often kick off. One time Charlie lost it with Dodi (the guy who went on to drive me and Ruel Fox to Tottenham training) for sparking up a cigarette mid-game while their team was losing. After an exchange of words, he marched off to his car, delved in the boot and came back waving a machete. Those guys would always encourage me to play, but my answer was always 'no way!' I couldn't get involved in all that as a young pro. The tackles were crazy.

Going back to Kieron, like everyone else, I thought, 'Wow, this boy is electric.' He was playing down the right side and we had a great relationship. He'd run and I'd spin him in. Quick, explosive, good on the ball – you just knew he wouldn't be there long. There was also Titus Bramble, whose dad I also remembered from playing in those Christchurch Park battles. Titus was only 16 at that time. He was another one where I thought 'what a player'. Strong, left foot, right foot, could head, he could play. It was great to see those two Ipswich boys going on to do well in the Premier League.

When you think about it, it's incredible that a town of this size has produced so many top-flight footballers over the years. There was Colin Harper and Brian Talbot, followed by me, Ruel Fox and Richard Hall, then Richard Wright, Dyer and Bramble. Now, of course, Ipswich boys Luke Woolfenden, Harry Clarke and Cameron Humphreys have joined that list, while my boy Andre still hopes of getting to the Premier League. That's not even mentioning those from wider Suffolk like Gavin Johnson, Matt Upson and James Scowcroft, or those who had or now have good Football League careers like Luke Hyam, Ian Brown, Liam Trotter, Ed Upson and Macauley Bonne. We do turn them out for one reason or another.

After that Manchester United game the *Ipswich Evening Star* published a petition that week urging the club to sign me up. I was thinking 'I'm in here', but it wasn't to be. After scoring in a 2-0 home win against Bury – my first Ipswich goal since that brace against Norwich four and a half years earlier – we had Birmingham away in midweek. I came off at half-time in that game ill, didn't train for the rest of the week, but still got picked at Charlton that weekend. I just didn't feel right and had to come off after half an hour. That night I went out for a quiet meal with my wife. That then got relayed back to the club that I'd been spotted out drinking. Someone had written in saying they'd heard me slagging George off. George called me in and showed me the letter. None of it was true and I told him that.

I played a few more games and scored at Oxford with a great header, which gave me hope of a new deal, but then two days later I got a shock at training. The usual list was up on the wall outlining who'd be travelling that weekend and my name wasn't on it. I was down to train with the goalkeepers. *What's going on here?* After training I was told to go and see George at the ground. That's when I knew something was wrong. All these young players were in the squad to travel and I wasn't. It was a gut-wrenching feeling. On that journey from Bent Lane to Portman Road I felt like a dead man walking.

George told me my short-term contract wasn't getting extended. He did it gently. He explained he had 'James

Scowcroft coming back from injury and some other good young players coming through whose pathways he didn't want to block. Looking back, I get it. That's football. I didn't take it well at the time, though. It was in that meeting that the penny dropped about my off-field reputation and how I was now going to pay for that. I don't think the letter sent in, which I reiterate was nonsense, was the reason I was let go, but it probably didn't help. I did a lot of shouting about that. Deep down, I was angry with myself. At Tottenham I had gone out far too much. People talk. It gets about. I had created this reputation.

Maybe Ipswich only ever saw me as short-term cover, but I thought, at the age of 29, I genuinely had something more to offer. I thought I would go full circle and play another 100-plus games for my hometown club. Having experienced what it was like to be thrust into the limelight at 16, I thought I could help some of these boys of a similar age early in their careers. Whether people in the club thought I was a bad influence on them, I don't know. I didn't socialise with the young players though and I tried to give them good advice about what to do and not do at the training ground.

I watched on enviously as my beloved Blues went on to finish fifth, third and third, eventually sealing promotion via the play-offs in 2000. I carried a lot of resentment about not being part of that for quite some time.

The day I got released by Ipswich was the day my love of football died. Yes, I played for a few more years, but a light went out when that association was over.

17

Falling Out of Love With the Game

I WENT on a hell of a bender the night that George Burley told me I was being let go by Ipswich. Then I woke up the next morning and thought, 'You need to do something or you're going to be in trouble.' I was heartbroken, but I knew I couldn't wallow in self-pity.

Within a couple of hours I got a phone call from Ian Atkins, my old Ipswich team-mate who was the manager of Northampton. 'Come and play for me,' he said. I wasn't sure. They'd just come up from the bottom rung of the English football pyramid.

But then Ian offered me a hell of a deal. I can't remember the exact wage, but it was something like four grand a week. That was good money in those days, as much as I had been on at Ipswich. I jumped on it because I didn't want to be waiting about. I couldn't sit around thinking about stuff.

What a fall from grace 1997 had been. I'd started the year having been given assurances that Tottenham wanted to give me a new contract. In May, I'd started a Premier League game at Liverpool. In October, I'd been man of the match against

Manchester United for my top-flight-chasing hometown club. Come November, however, I found myself a third-tier player preparing to face the likes of Walsall, York and Wrexham.

My spell with the Cobblers was a familiar story. Again, a month-to-month deal. Again, I started off on fire, scoring three goals in my first five games. Again, there was a petition from the fans to get me to sign for longer. This time I did put pen to paper until the end of the season – but then I dipped dramatically.

Living in Ipswich, I was travelling an hour and 45 there, an hour and 45 back for training every day. Then, come the weekend, I was getting kicked all over the place on the pitch. It was all aerial duels in the midfield and I was constantly coming off with black eyes. Dropping from the Premier League to the Second Division so quickly was a culture shock. I was no longer playing in big stadiums. The football was just crap. My legs had started to go. I could feel everything wasn't quite functioning right.

It was a slog. I was tired. I just wasn't enjoying it. The bubble had burst. I tried to love the game still, but it was a fight. My God, it became a grind.

Come March and April, I didn't make the starting XI a few times. I got back in though and a 1-0 win at Fulham, followed by a 0-0 draw at York on the final day, saw us secure a play-off spot. Back-to-back promotions were on.

We faced Bristol Rovers in the semis. I played in the first leg at the Memorial Stadium. Ronnie Mauge, a fellow Ipswich boy, completely man-marked me out the game. He did not leave my side and did a proper job on me. We lost 3-1.

I didn't even make the bench for the second leg and watched on as we turned the tie around with an incredible 3-0 win to set up a Wembley final. I should have been buzzing. There was a chance, 13 years on from that Milk Cup semi-final heartbreak with Ipswich, for me to play under the famous Twin Towers. Very few players get to do that in their careers. I know that. Honestly though, I didn't feel an awful lot. That's where my head was at.

Come the final I was lucky to be on the bench. We lost 1-0 to Grimsby in front of a crowd of more than 60,000 – a record attendance for that fixture at the time – with close to three-quarters of those fans backing Northampton. I was the only one of our three subs not to get on. I couldn't complain either. I didn't deserve to be on the pitch because my form had dipped massively. Getting released came as no surprise. Once more, I found myself a free agent.

I was starting not to like myself at that time. I think that process began when George had told me, 'Jason, you know there's a stigma now?' That's when the penny dropped. I was now seen as a bad egg. I knew I wasn't a bad egg in terms of the changing room, but I was only just starting to realise that you will get judged by people who haven't spent one minute in your company. Sadly, that's the world we live in.

After that I went to Gillingham on trial with Paul Mason, who had just left Ipswich. They'd just finished narrowly outside the play-off places in the Second Division and had Tony Pulis as manager. I played one practice game – it was intense, battles everywhere – and I thought, 'No, fuck this.' That feeling probably went both ways, to be fair.

Tony probably took one look at me and thought exactly the same.

I didn't want to go far from Ipswich, so my pool of potential clubs was small. Unsurprisingly, I ended up signing for Colchester with all my mates. They'd just come up from the Third Division. My old going out partner Steve Whitton was assistant manager, and later became manager, while there were a few other ex-Ipswich boys in the squad. George Williams and the Gregory brothers, David and Neil, were there when I arrived, while Gavin Johnson and Adam Tanner later joined. We had some great times socially, but the football – again, that was hard work. Layer Road was a rum old ground.

When I signed for Colchester I started to learn about how much bad feeling had been created by George Burley walking away from them to join Ipswich on Christmas Eve in '94. Colchester–Ipswich – they think that's a rivalry. I didn't. But I soon saw that they really hate us. I'd go out for a few drinks and their fans would be on me as a former Ipswich player. I was confused. I was thinking, 'You're not my rival, Norwich is my rival.' It could get quite intense on nights out in Colchester because, as a garrison town, you'd have all the squaddies around and they don't mess about. I felt edgy as anything. I didn't hang around for long if I felt something brewing.

I scored at Manchester City in my third game for Colchester, pulling a goal back in a 2-1 defeat against Joe Royle's men. I always seemed to score at Maine Road. They went on to secure promotion in dramatic fashion that season, Paul Dickov's late goal against Gillingham in the play-off final going down in club folklore. I do remember them coming down to little Layer Road late in that campaign and finding that tough, though.

I've spoken a lot in this book about how much I loved the FA Cup, from watching the '78 final as a young fan to scoring plenty of goals in it for Ipswich as a player. My relationship with the world-famous competition, sadly, ended on a bit of a sour note with Colchester, however.

In November 1998, we drew non-league club Bedlington Terriers in the first round. It had all the ingredients for an upset. We had a long journey to Northumberland, they were flying in their league, we weren't going great in ours and the weather was foul. The playing surface was terrible, but they played like Brazil that day. I've been popped before on a football pitch, but that was against teams like Manchester United. This was Bedlington Terriers! I just couldn't run in the mud. People were running off me for fun. I got subbed at half-time when we were 2-0 down, we lost the game 4-1 and suffered the ignominy of a big billing on *Match of the Day* that night. That was probably the day when I first properly thought, 'Get me out of this.'

You keep going though and you get through it. You have to, because you've got no choice. My wages had taken a big drop and I'd not saved as well as I should have. This was now well and truly just a job to pay the bills. I tried to do as well as I could, and we had some great games along the way, but deep down I knew it was coming to an end. I wasn't feeling good.

It was around the time of that Bedlington defeat that word started going around about this young player the club had just signed – Lomana LuaLua. I think he'd been spotted playing college football and Steve Wignall, the manager, was clearly excited by this hidden gem that had been uncovered.

Lomana only started playing football at 16. He was just a street footballer, very, very raw, but you could tell he had that X-factor. He loved me because I used to give him the ball all the time. I'd then stand back and watch him beat three or four men for fun, score and then run off and do six or seven somersaults in celebration. An outstanding hat-trick at QPR in the League Cup took him to new heights in the early stages of the 2000/01 season. Mick Wadsworth, who had become assistant manager at Newcastle after resigning from his role as Colchester boss, played a part in his £2.25m switch to St James' Park. The best person Lomana could have gone to work with was Bobby Robson. It was no surprise to me to see his talents subsequently harnessed in the Premier League.

Thanks to YouTube there is one moment from my three years at Colchester that people always ask about. Google my name and a video comes up entitled 'Jason Dozzell misses a sitter'. The grainy footage from a home game against Notts County on 16 April 1999 begins with the commentator saying, 'Coming up, one of those moments where you ask "how did he miss?"' He's not wrong. I'm no more than a yard out at the back post, but I shovel the ball back across goal and allow the keeper to make a save. My boys take great delight in showing me that one back at least once a week. I always maintain that it crossed the line! Where was VAR when I needed it?!

Midway through my second season at Colchester, Steve Whitton brought in an 18-year-old Titus Bramble on loan from Ipswich. I'd trained with him a bit when I went back there in 1997, so I knew what we were getting. Titus only played two games during that one-month spell, but he was sensational. I can still picture one run at Blackpool from his own half where he nearly went all the way. OK, he gave away a penalty in the next one with the most blatant foul you've ever seen, but you could see he was a beast.

Towards the start of the 2000/01 season, Colchester were on the end of another FA Cup upset – a 5-1 loss at Yeovil. This time I lasted an hour before getting the hook. It's the worst feeling when you're coming towards the end of your career. Those two years when you know it's coming, when your body can no longer do what it used to, when you know you're not the player you used to be – it's horrible. Every ex-player will tell you that.

Even now I don't play football. I hate it. Your reactions are gone. I'm in my 50s, I shouldn't worry about it, but it's a nightmare for me. I see Johnny Wark is still playing now in his 60s and loving it. Fair play, but personally I can't think of anything worse.

I was only 30 when I signed for Colchester, but I already had a 14-year playing career behind me. Most players don't get into the first team regularly until they are at least 20 and retire at 34 or 35. I started at 16 and had racked up the same mileage much sooner. Did I have my peak at 25, instead of 29 or 30, as a result? Probably. My legs definitely went earlier than most. Those last few years were a real struggle.

It's no surprise that things caught up with me physically. We sometimes played two games in two days in the '80s, which seems ridiculous now. The sports science and nutrition wasn't there. Recovery was just a cold bath. Come the start of the 2000s, I was really feeling it.

On Boxing Day 2001, I played in a 6-1 defeat at Millwall. I didn't know it at the time, but that would be my final game of professional football. A joint on the side of my foot had caused me grief for ages. Eventually I had an operation, but it didn't sort it out. That was that. I retired at 33. 'I'm gutted' was the quote in the newspapers the next day. In truth, it was a relief.

Even though that moment had been coming for a while, I hadn't given one thought to what I'd do next. Ipswich had pulled me out of school before I'd finished my exams at 16. All I'd known was football. So, despite not enjoying the game, I eked out another year in non-league.

Glenn Pennyfather, another of my former Ipswich teammates, persuaded me to go and join him at Canvey Island alongside Neil Gregory. I didn't pull up any trees. Most of the time I felt I was the worst player on the pitch. The football was, again, so different to what I was used to. It was even more physical than what I'd experienced at Northampton and Colchester. I seemed to be a target and got kicked all over the place.

I'd never been sent off before in my career, but in my first game in non-league I was given my marching orders for some verbals. The referee didn't take a liking to me and, in colourful terms, I called him a cheat. That was a sign of my frustrations. I didn't last at Canvey very long, no more than a couple of months. After that I went to Grays Athletic and it was a similar story. Just one appearance there. There was just nothing left.

A much happier spell followed when I got offered the player-manager's job at Ipswich Wanderers. Just being at a club with the name 'Ipswich' lifted me. I felt a connection there. It felt like being home. When Ipswich Town were away, loads of fans would come to watch us. We got some big crowds. That was nice.

My management style mirrored what I'd experienced as a player. Off the field, as had been the case in that promotion season at Ipswich, a big emphasis was put on togetherness socially. We created a close bond. On the training pitch, mimicking what I enjoyed under Ossie at Spurs, it was all off the cuff. There were lots of five-a-sides and not much talk about the opposition. I'd drum it into the players that they needed to look after the ball. I told them there was going to be no bypassing of the midfield with me there. It may have been non-league, but I was going to make them play.

I played myself at centre-half. My legs may have gone, but I could still read the game. Rather than diving into tackles, I would intercept then roll it into someone's feet. I speak to some of those players now. They say, 'You used to play the ball to me in tight areas and I was shitting myself, but after a while I got used to it.' Eventually, we started to play some nice stuff.

In my second season, we won the league title and got promoted to the Eastern Counties League Premier Division. I was really proud of that. The following season we finished seventh, the highest the club had ever been in the pyramid, but that wasn't enough to keep my job. They suddenly had big ambitions and I didn't fit with those. They'd drawn up all these plans for a new clubhouse and someone came in with money. Players went from being on £30 or £40 a game to £200 a game. You see it a lot in non-league. People come in with money, they want to have a say in the football side of things, make a load of changes, then two years later they disappear.

After that I got the manager's job at Leiston. We finished fifth in the Eastern Counties League Premier Division, above Ipswich Wanderers, but just a few months into the following season I was out of the door there too. Out of the blue, they told me they wanted a manager who was going to take a more hands-on role with the youth team and the reserves. I couldn't really be more interactive on that front because Andre was starting to play academy football at Ipswich and I needed to give him some focus.

It seemed like it was going to be a pretty amicable parting of ways until we got on to the financials. I had a contract until the end of the season and they were refusing to pay up. This went on for weeks and we weren't getting anywhere. In the end I took matters into my own hands. I picked up the phone to the chairman and played a card I'd always used in times of trouble.

'Right, I've called my complaints department and we're coming over tomorrow.' I never had to use the name Tony Swallow explicitly for people to know what that meant. I put the phone down and 30 seconds later I got a call back. 'OK, there's no need for that, I'll meet you in the car park at Woodbridge Football Club with the money.' When I got there, it wasn't just the three grand I was owed in that envelope but also an extra few hundred for goodwill. I hadn't actually spoken to Tony. That was a lie. I shouldn't have done that, but he wasn't going to pay up and there was no reason why he shouldn't.

I didn't get back into non-league after that. For the first time in my adult life, I wasn't part of a football dressing room. That was always going to be problematic for me.

18

Slow Descent to a Dark Place

I KEEP having this same dream where I score the winner in the FA Cup Final at Wembley. Everything happens in glorious slow motion. I'm in complete control. The most intense feeling of joy surges through my body as the ball hits the back of the net. The colours, the sounds, the smells – it's all so vivid, so real.

And then I wake up. *Where am I?* It takes a couple of seconds for reality to hit. *Fuck.* That crushing disappointment never, ever lessens. If anything, it gets worse.

I lived for those intense highs and sensory overloads. When you walk out the tunnel for a big game, the two teams side-by-side, and that roar goes up – the hairs on the back of my neck go up thinking about that. When you score a winner in front of tens of thousands of people and there's that split second of silence followed by an explosion of noise – that was almost an out-of-body experience.

It's not just those big moments I miss either. Just not being in the changing room every day, laughing with the boys, leaves a huge void too. When you retire all that is gone. Nothing can match it.

That cup final dream is telling me a story. It's telling me that football is my life. It's telling me that not only do I miss playing terribly, but that, more than anything, I miss those adrenaline spikes.

For some footballers, retirement is great. Some can put their career in a box, slow down and enjoy family life. Not me. I wasn't wired that way. For me, retirement was the start of the chaos. My mind went into overdrive.

It felt like my football career had gone by in the blink of an eye. Training, playing, partying – from the age of 16 to when I retired, I never had time to stop and think. Then when I did stop it was like, 'What just happened?' It felt as if I was looking back on a different person.

Reflections on the football were secondary. The first remorse was about my babies' mother. 'God, my wife' was the emotion that hit me hardest. I have got a heart and it went straight there. She loved me a hell of a lot and I'm just sorry I wasn't able to give her that love back in the same way. She wouldn't know this, but thinking about what I'd done to her was one of the key factors in sending me downwards.

I've never wanted to be horrible or thought of myself that way, but I had this moment of realisation that I had turned into a selfish person. I'd always done what I wanted to do and never thought about the consequences. I felt entitled and that's wrong. I looked back and saw that I didn't handle things at all well when I went to London. I should have spoken to my wife about that, once I'd had that moment of self-reflection, but I didn't. I couldn't.

My relationship with Leonie had always been on-off. She'd leave me and then come back. I was living with someone else post playing career when she said 'I still love you'. There was too much water under the bridge, I was thinking 'this isn't going to work', but we got back together again and I got another lovely son in Emile. Unfortunately, I was soon back to my old ways. When I went out, sometimes I didn't get home. That was the problem. That's not nice for anyone.

Why, after feeling all that guilt, didn't I take my second chance to settle down? I don't know. Most people get to the middle ground in life and can be content. For some reason, I can never find contentment. It's like I find comfort in the chaos. I've always got to be up or down.

I just wasn't stimulated. A normal, steady home life with the wife and kids just wasn't doing it for me. I'd have a great week and then Friday would come along and I'd start getting fidgety and edgy. I don't even know I'm doing it, but every girl I've been with has recognised it. They knew I needed to get out and unwind and do what I needed to do for me.

I'm painting it like I was a monster. I wasn't a monster. I had some fantastic times with Leonie – great holidays, days out in London. We were together a long time, so I couldn't have been all that bad. All I can say is that it's the bad things that stick in my mind. The things that I am not proud of override the rest of my memories. It's the same with my football. I am working on that.

Eventually, we got divorced. The past just caught up on us. I didn't get kicked out. I made the decision to leave in the best interests of our children.

I need to big Leonie up here. My kids are fantastic people and that's all down to her. She's done all the everyday hard yards with them. School runs, looking after them when they've been ill, all that sort of stuff. I've got so much respect for her and so much respect for single mums full stop.

Thoughts rattled around in my head. *What happened to that nice 16-year-old boy? Where's he gone? When did you change? Why did you change? Was it the money? Was it the attention? Why couldn't you handle it better? Is this my real personality?* You're trying to join the dots, but that's impossible if the page is black. That's how I felt for about 20 years of my life. Just lost.

Time will make you think. Self-doubt starts to creep in and self-doubt will keep you awake at night. Boredom too. It all contributes to your mental health. I was out of my comfort zone.

If you don't like yourself you can't go forward. Once I started thinking 'you're not what you think you are, this behaviour is not great' it sent me towards a dark place. Then you repeat that behaviour as some strange act of self-punishment.

In September 2004, three years after retirement, I was disqualified from driving for 12 months after failing to provide a specimen. I'd just come back from London, I'd only had two pints and I'd had nothing to eat. I panicked when they stopped me and got the breathalyser out. That was stupid.

Three years later, in December 2007, I turned 40. That milestone, coming fresh off a divorce, just intensified all the feelings of self-loathing. Two days before Christmas I went to Portman Road to watch Ipswich draw 0-0 with Burnley and then met some friends afterwards. It turned into a proper session. I just wanted to escape my own head.

Come the early hours of the morning I remembered I'd left my car in not the most secure car park around the back end of the docks. I'd had cars stolen and keyed overnight before so, idiotically, I decided to go and move it.

When I saw the police car behind me on the one-way system, again I panicked. I eventually pulled into Cardinal Park and awaited the tap on my window. I couldn't believe who I saw next; it was Murray Osman. Murray is Russell Osman's brother and I'd played with him in the youth team at Ipswich. But now he's a copper. The irony wasn't lost on me. One of the highest points in my life had involved a car and an Osman, now one of the lowest points did too. He had a sad, apologetic look as he dealt with me. I must have looked pathetic. It was a really awkward moment between the two of us.

This time I submitted to the breathalyser test without complaint and blew almost two times over the limit. A couple of weeks later I appeared in South East Suffolk Magistrates' Court and sat there feeling utterly numb as the prosecutor read out witness statements describing me being 'unsteady on his feet' and 'swerving through a no entry sign'. They hit me with a three-year ban.

It's really important here that I get this message across – drink-driving is absolutely stupid. Everybody did it years ago – I'm not going to name names – but that doesn't make it right. There are no excuses at all. I know what the consequences could be. I could have killed someone. I got it wrong with cars, it's ridiculous what I've done, and I just want to make that very clear. You deserve everything you get when you're over the limit.

At that stage, I was out of control. I was frustrated with life and frustrated with myself. I didn't realise it at the time, but I was on a slow descent to a dark place.

* * *

I had things going on in my life that should have made me happy and content.

After retirement, I got selected to play beach football for England in Marbella. I don't know why they picked me, but off I went with Ruel Fox, Des Walker and some other big hitters. Me and Foxy went out on the first night and didn't get back until silly o'clock. As we staggered into the hotel, the Spanish players passed us in the lobby. They were heading out for an early morning training session. It was at that very moment that it dawned on us we were playing them in just a few hours' time. Foxy and I looked at each other as if to say, 'we're in trouble here'. The game kicked off at 2pm, the hottest part of the day, and we were 2-0 down after 20 seconds. This geezer ran off me, did an overhead kick and put the ball top bins. Hungover, temperature above 100 degrees, running on sand, playing against the Spanish – I think that's the worst I've ever felt, physically, on a football pitch. It was horrific!

I played Masters football for Ipswich and England too. I went to Ireland for one tournament and Canada for another. When it first started it was older blokes with beer bellies running around and having a laugh. Ipswich won it the first year. We were the new boys and most of us were just on that 35 years old button playing against people like Glenn Hoddle, who is ten years older than me. There were no more 45-plus-year-olds selected after that though. People started picking younger and younger players. It got silly competitive. That side of it wasn't for me, but at least I got a few good trips out of it.

When I retired, I looked into coaching and realised you've got to do all these courses. I was thinking, 'They took me out of school, so why do I now have to do all this?' There was no way I was going back in the classroom. Why should I? I had that mentality. I had my own soccer school for a spell, that was flying, then my son Andre joined the Ipswich Town academy at under-ten level and all of a sudden the club was saying, 'Come and work for us.' I never needed any qualifications then.

I started off coaching the under-12s and I loved it. I moved all the way through – 13s, 14s, 15s, 16s and eventually up to the 18s and a bit of 21s. Always in the back of my head though I was thinking, 'I'm only here because of Andre.'

There's lots and lots of computer work in academies now, every session has to be planned and then logged, but I couldn't do it. I'm not embarrassed to say it, I hate that kind of stuff. It makes me uncomfortable and nervous. No one else would have got that job without being able to do all that, but they seemed to turn a blind eye to it with me because of Andre. The poor coach I worked alongside always had to do all the paperwork.

I wouldn't say I'm a great coach, but I've got great knowledge of the game. It's weird. I can't sit at home or in an office and come up with a session. I need to be on the football pitch to get my head right. It's only when I get to Playford

Road or Portman Road that my mind starts going. It's visual with me. I need to be on the pitch to see the picture and then be able to pass that on. A lot of people can go on the laptop and design a session, but they won't necessarily give the in-session detail. My strength, as a former player, would be to spot when something wasn't right. 'Stop the game. Let's think about how that unfolded.'

As a player, I was very good when it came to anticipation and thinking about the second pass. It's easy to anticipate that the first pass is going out to the wing, but where is the next player going to play the ball? As soon as that ball is played wide, as a midfield player you need to start making your run into the box anticipating the cross. Don't start that run when the winger controls the ball, make it before the ball even gets to them. Anticipate the second pass, not the first. That's the difference between getting there or not. It's like playing chess. You've got to think several moves ahead.

Another strength of mine was playing on the half turn and playing forward. Whenever I think 'he's a good player' it's because they pass forward. That's always what I look for. If someone can receive the ball on the half turn, turn and go forwards, for me that's good play. A lot of players always knock it sideways or backwards because their body shape is not right. So what I used to say to them is that when they're receiving, always give themselves three options: one, to go back to where it came from; two, to go sideways; and three, to go forward. That means you're going to have to be on the half turn. That's my thing. Let me see, by your body shape, that you always give yourself the option to play around the corner and go forwards.

Phil Foden is the best at it. Receive on the half turn, spin and drive. It's not natural to everybody, but it's important.

In the academy there are four corners you've got to hit – technical, physical, psychological and social. I tried to hit all of them in every session I did. Social is working together as a team, technical is the stuff I've just said – see the picture, play on the half turn – while physically I'd make it tough. Psychologically you're looking out for how they react when 3-0 down in a little five-a-side game. Do they give up? Who's going to be the leader?

Working alongside Adem Atay with the under-21s was a great journey. These boys were the cream of the crop. When things came off in the games that we'd worked on during the week it gave me huge satisfaction. I didn't just work on them with the football, I got to know them as people too. I spoke to them about their families, their hobbies, asked them how they were feeling. They need to know you care. We got to the semi-finals of the FA Youth Cup in 2021, eventually losing narrowly to Liverpool. I think the scenes in the dressing room after the extra-time quarter-final win against Sheffield United, which the club filmed and put out, showed what those boys thought of me.

Working in the academy made me think about my own start in football. I joined Ipswich at 14, trained on a Thursday night for two hours and was suddenly thrust into the limelight with all the dangers that brings. These days an academy product is carefully cultivated from the age of eight or nine. The young lads have so much structure. They don't just get coached to be good players, but they are helped to become good people as well. They get help with their education, have access to sports psychologists, get media training, financial advice and are warned about the potential pitfalls ahead. Maybe if I'd have had the benefits of all that then things would have been different for me.

Then again, if I hadn't been given the freedom to be kicked from pillar to post at the park, enjoying the game pressure-free until a later age, maybe I wouldn't have become the player I did either. It's hard to say. I don't see enough young players now with that street mentality.

I could always see the difference when we played some of the London teams. Their players looked streetwise, while our Ipswich boys looked nice. I'm not saying nice boys can't make it, they can, but I do think you've got to have that little bit of nastiness, selfishness, arrogance – whatever you want to call it – to go really high. Players like Wayne Rooney and Steven Gerrard had that. They went over to the first team at 16, 17, and kicked lumps out of the senior players. I'm going to hit you hard, no matter who you are. That's the mentality that's needed.

It was great seeing Andre progress alongside Luke Woolfenden because they had started out in the same St Johns under-eight team. I hear a lot of people say that Flynn Downes was a late developer, but I always knew there was something with him. The good thing about Flynn is he doesn't complicate his game. He's no frills. He wins it, gives it. He can cover distances. That is a modern Premier League player.

Ben Knight would be up there as one of the best I worked with. Manchester City lured him away in 2018, but he doesn't seem to have kicked on. You see it all the time. You get thrivers at 12 years old who, come 16, are strugglers. Conversely, you get strugglers at 12 who, come 16, are thrivers. You develop when you're ready to develop. Until they're filled out physically you can't judge. It's only at 16 that they're on an equal playing field.

The game is definitely changing. You've got to be an outstanding technical player if you're a little dot. There isn't much room for them any more. They're all big, strong, athletic. That is the DNA of an academy player now, whereas before one of the first things they were looking for was, 'Can you receive it on the back foot?' I think it's athletes first now and 'can we improve them as footballers?' after. If you're 6ft 3in and can get about the pitch, clubs will take you over the technical boys. That's the way it's going.

* * *

For ten years or so, I thought I was functioning OK. I enjoyed the coaching, Andre was progressing, I had girlfriends here and there.

I had a settled period with one girl. Cathy was another one who loved me to bits. She provided me with structure, three meals a day, but the same kinds of patterns were playing out. I was brilliant during the week, but selfish come the weekends.

What was I searching for? What did I want? I don't know, but that self-destructive behaviour was always going to catch up with me at some point.

19

History Repeats

I VIVIDLY remember getting the phone call from my wife saying she was pregnant. I was in Singapore with Tottenham on an end-of-season trip. It was brilliant news. Obviously, I went out celebrating with the lads.

My first son, Dion, was born on 30 December 1995. I was out drinking when I got a phone call about one in the morning from Leonie saying, 'Get your arse home, the baby is coming!' I was absolutely steaming. I got home and she had to drive us to the hospital. He was three weeks early, to be fair! They had to put the gas thing on me because I nearly passed out. He eventually arrived about mid-morning just as my hangover was kicking in.

Dion didn't start playing football until he was ten. He was at the likes of Whitton, Woodbridge and Holbrook growing up, then went off on a soccer scholarship in the US at 18 – North Iowa first and then Florida. Fair play to him, I couldn't have done that. I didn't worry about him at all, though. He's just got that personality where he can go and fit in anywhere. He's a great kid.

At one stage he kept sending me videos of all these incredible goals he was scoring and I was thinking, 'Is that really you?' This went on for a long time. I was close to giving Ipswich a call and saying 'have a look at this' because he was absolutely flying. Then he suffered an ACL injury and, as soon as he got back from that, Covid came. He got disrupted badly.

Now he's back working in London but setting up a company in Miami. It's for high-end footballers who want to do some individual warm-weather training in the off-season. They sort out the hotels, the cars, the training facilities, restaurants, everything. Footballers' summers are a bit different to what they were in my day!

My second son, Andre, was born on 2 May 1999 when I was a Colchester player. I was out with him with the ball quite early on. He played for St Johns and several of his friends got into Ipswich first. He must have been thinking 'what's going on here?' because he was better than the others. Then St Johns played Ipswich at Playford Road in a practice game and he just smashed it. They snapped him up straight after that. Seeing him put on that Ipswich kit for the first time was something else.

I was a bad parent on the sideline. When Andre was in the under-nines they were getting beat 9-0 at Arsenal and the coaches were just standing there doing nothing. I now know it's because they were letting the players try and work it out for themselves, but at the time I thought they just didn't care. It used to wind me up. You're not supposed to, but I was stood there trying to dictate the game. I was thinking,

'They're 9-0 down, they need help!' I got called in after that and reprimanded. They said, 'Just be a parent, let us coach, we have a way.' Once I got in the building as an academy coach myself, I started to understand how they worked.

After that it was years of watching Andre grow. It was obvious early on that he had a talent. When we sat and watched *Match of the Day* together, he'd rather talk about the playmakers than the goalscorers. When he played, while all the other young kids wanted to dribble and score, he was content passing. It was just beautiful to watch his progression, but I always kept grounded because I'd seen so many young players fade over the years. Andre just kept thriving, though.

At 16, he got his scholarship and by the end of that first year he was called up to first-team training by Mick McCarthy ahead of a Championship game at Sheffield Wednesday. I was working in the academy at that time, so I went up to Mick and said, 'Can you let me know if he's going to be on the bench, because if he is I'll have to cancel training tomorrow.' Mick told me, 'Yeah, he's going to be on the bench,' so I made plans. I wasn't expecting him to get on, but I wanted to be there for a big moment in his career.

I travelled up to Hillsborough the next day with a few mates. We watched the first half, Ipswich went 1-0 behind and I went down for a pie at half-time. Then, as I walked back up the steps into the stands, I caught a glimpse of the dugouts. There he was, stood on the sidelines stripped and ready to come on. *Wow.* The hairs on the back of my neck stood up. It was like I was instantly transported back to my own debut in February 1984.

Ipswich rode their luck. They should have gone 2-0 down. Then, in the 71st minute, Tommy Smith dribbled out from the back and played a pass up the line. Kevin Bru gave the ball to Andre and he worked it out to the left. *Go on son, get in the box, do something monstrous.* Time then seemed to go in slow motion as Liam Feeney crossed. Andre timed his run to perfection, getting between two defenders to send a header high into the net from six yards out.

I didn't believe in fate until then. How could I not after that, though? I scored on my debut for Ipswich Town, my hometown club, as a sub, aged 16. Now, 32 years later, my son had done exactly the same. The Town fans were going mad around me. I was crying with joy. That was just an incredible moment.

As a sidenote, I felt a bit for my mate that day. He'd tried to put money on Andre scoring, but Andre wasn't on the bookie's squad list so they couldn't take the bet. I don't know what price he would have been, but it would have been a decent payout.

That day is one Andre and I often talk about. I'm sure we'll continue to do so long after he's retired too. I can imagine his son, who's only little now, will get very tired of hearing the tale. 'Yes granddad [I still can't get used to being called that], I know, dad was nearly 17 and you had only just turned 16.' I'm always quick to remind Andre of that if he ever gets a bit lairy!

Andre first got in the England youth set up at under-16 level. When he'd join up with the squad at St George's Park there'd be four players from Manchester United, four from Liverpool, four from Arsenal. It's cliquey and young boys today can be quite ruthless. That wasn't easy for this little boy from Ipswich to deal with.

'Stand tall, stick out your chest, go and get their respect on the pitch,' I told him. He did just that and they kept on picking him. Going away on foreign trips to watch him was amazing because, unlike in Ipswich, I could walk freely wherever I wanted and no one knew me. It meant I didn't have to speak to anyone. It was beautiful.

As my slow descent into a dark place started, watching Andre became my sanctuary. How he was doing played a big part in how I felt. Tying so many of my own personal emotions up in him, in hindsight, probably wasn't healthy.

After he'd made a handful of appearances for the Ipswich first team in 2016/17, Andre went away with England under-19s, a year group up, and played a key role in them winning the European Championship in Georgia. The likes of Reece James and Mason Mount were in that side. That was magical.

He came back flying that summer. In the first Championship game of the season, at home against Birmingham, he started and was having a blinder. Then he jumped, landed awkwardly and had to be stretchered off. Bang – ACL injury. He'd had everything going his way, was on a constant upwards trajectory, but then suddenly had that all snatched away. I told him, 'That's how football goes son, you will be back.'

When Andre did his knee, I went to see him at his mum's house the next day and Mick McCarthy turned up out the blue to see how he was, which was a lovely touch. I loved Mick. He always spoke to me and was always polite.

The first bit of transfer interest in Andre came from Liverpool when he was 16. Those talks actually got quite advanced. We went to Anfield and had a meeting. My feeling was it was too early for a move like that, but you have to remember that Ipswich was a funny club at that time. It was just starting to struggle. Liverpool said, 'You might not get in the team for a while, but you're going to get coached well.' Ultimately it was Andre's decision and he said, 'No, I want to play for my hometown club.' I was relieved.

Just like me, Andre came through at a difficult time for the club under a manager who was playing pragmatic, percentage football. Going from England to playing for Mick McCarthy – that transition was massive for him. The playing philosophies were completely different. I told him, 'Be really good at what you're good at, don't ever lose that, because there will always be someone who will take you for that.' But I also encouraged him to work on other bits of his game too. It reminded me so much of my time under John Duncan.

I had a few years where things were all right. Then I don't know why, but I just started getting lower and lower. What were the triggers? I think seeing things not go quite as planned for Andre was a big one. I don't know if that's an excuse or not. It was definitely becoming difficult watching Andre trying to make it at a struggling club, though. I wasn't enjoying that. I'm an Ipswich fan, now I've got my boy there and it's not going the way it was for him pre-ACL injury. That was hard.

Paul Hurst replaced McCarthy in the summer of 2018. When he arrived, he said all the right things about wanting to work with academy players. That pre-season ended with a game against West Ham at Portman Road in which Andre, Luke Woolfenden, Flynn Downes and Tristan Nydam all started. All aged between 18 and 19, they looked fearless against Premier League stars. They were combining and doing all sorts. We may have lost 2-1 in the end, but what a feeling everyone had after that game.

It wasn't long before Hurst said something in the paper along the lines of, 'Why's Andre Dozzell been put on this pedestal?' I don't think he needed to say that. I thought that was out of order. 'He doesn't deserve to be in there' – in my mind, that's what he was really trying to say. Then he took Andre out of the first-team changing room and put him with the under-23s. It was a terrible time.

Luke Woolfenden and Tristan Nydam were loaned out towards the end of that window, with Flynn Downes sent away in the January. It's such a shame the club was how it was when that crop of homegrown players all came of age. If that had been now, under Kieran McKenna, with the club on the up, they would have thrived together, I'm sure. It was just the wrong time. They were coming into a team in decline and there's nothing worse for young players than that. I know, because I'd experienced that myself.

Am I jealous that things have taken off since Andre left? Of course I am. Kieran McKenna has improved every single one of those players. There are players in the team now who a few years ago, being blunt, I thought were horrific. That is the art of coaching. It's all about making people feel good. How things could have been for Andre if he'd come through under McKenna, playing in front of a packed Portman Road, is something I think about a lot.

Andre is best mates with Woolfy. You speak to Luke now and he's bubbly, but that wasn't always the case. I remember bumping into his mum when he had been cast aside for a spell. She told me how he had been in a bad place with his mental health. I remember reading an interview with him in the *East Anglian Daily Times* further down the line where he said there was a time when he just wanted to stay in bed and that his head was 'in the bin'. It's a reminder that footballers are human beings too. We're not robots. I'm so pleased to see Luke doing so well for the club now. It's great what he's doing.

Paul Hurst didn't last long. Paul Lambert came in and relegation to League One followed. Lambert didn't play Andre every game to start with, but then the owner, Marcus Evans, stepped in and said he didn't want a valuable asset to depreciate. Lambert was all right with Andre, to be fair, but a negative vibe around the club grew the longer they stayed in League One. Andre, just as was the case with me, started getting labelled a 'luxury player'. People were quick to highlight his weaknesses rather than his strengths.

I love Mick Mills, he was a brilliant captain for Ipswich and one of my heroes growing up, so it hurt to hear some of the things he said about Andre on the radio. I felt there were some personal attacks. I had pros ringing me up saying, 'What's Andre done to Mick Mills?' It happened a lot and it used to upset my weekend. I listened to it, I had to take it, but I didn't like it. I felt it wasn't needed for a young kid who had just come back from an ACL injury. As a proud father I guess you overthink stuff. I was disappointed. That's all I can say.

To me it felt like Andre's name was always the first to be criticised. In the end that's probably why he had to get out. The Dozzell name was going to cause him a problem. He almost left in 2019, to Norwich of all clubs, but I'll come on to that in the next chapter. That was a saga.

Andre had grown up hearing tales about his uncle Tony. I'd told him about my brother running on the pitch during games, going to war with Vinnie Jones, fighting the Tottenham fans and how I'd always had to be the peacemaker. He'd laugh, shake his head and say, 'How did you deal with that?' Well, unexpectedly, he got a little taste first-hand of what it was like in February 2021.

For a bit of background, Tony got a girl pregnant during the early '80s but she ended up moving to the US and their child was born and raised over there. That boy is Darnell Swallow. You might recognise the name. Darnell, who is an albino, appeared on reality TV show *Big Brother* in 2008 at the height of its popularity. He made headlines at the time for revealing in the house that he had once served time for drug dealing.

Fast forward more than a decade and larger-than-life Ipswich striker James Norwood was up to his usual antics on social media. Someone had a pop at him on Twitter and he came back at this guy, taking the piss out of his fair-skinned appearance and 'gap in your teeth' by attaching an unflattering image of Darnell. God knows how he'd plucked him out of the air. It was hardly a contemporary reference.

It wasn't long before my brother found out. He contacted me saying, 'We can't let this slide.' 'Just leave it Tone,' I told him. 'I know Norwood. He didn't mean anything by it. It was just footballers' banter.' Trust me, had that been several years earlier then James would have been in trouble, but thankfully Tony had mellowed a bit by then and I talked him down.

It wasn't long before people started pointing out to James that Darnell was, in actual fact, Andre's cousin and the sort of reputation his 'mad uncle Tony' had. He must have been sweating because the next post he put up was a picture of him and Andre smiling together at the team hotel. That little incident brought back some memories for me, let me tell you!

Andre signed a new three-year contract in December 2021 on the understanding that the club would sell him that summer if the right offer came along. Paul Cook replaced Paul Lambert in the March, and played Andre regularly, but said he wouldn't stand in his way. Paul obviously wanted to raise funds for his own dramatic squad rebuild following a limp finish to the season. Tony Mowbray was keen to take Andre to Blackburn, but he and his agent decided that QPR was the best option.

A couple of managers came and went at QPR, then Andre found himself playing under Gareth Ainsworth. Let's just say that, stylistically, it wasn't a great fit for him. I feared that he was going to get neckache watching the ball constantly go over his head in midfield. I watched him in one game against Watford and he did a brilliant man-marking job on João Pedro. Pedro's a top player, but he didn't get a kick that day. I noticed that Andre even man-for-manned him when QPR were in possession. 'Did the manager tell you to do that?' I asked him. 'Yeah,' he replied. I said, 'That's not you. You have to play to your strengths and the way you were brought up. If people don't like it, then you're just going to have to move on. I'm very proud of what you did, you worked your nuts off, but that's not who you are. Out of possession, fine, you have to do that. But in possession, you go and get the ball.'

I pointed out that he wasn't even going for throw-ins any more. 'The manager doesn't want me to because the throws are going long,' he explained. 'That's fine,' I said. 'But you still have to make a point of going to show for the ball because there is always someone watching you and they'll be thinking you don't want the ball otherwise. So check in, show for the ball and when it goes long then you push into the game. Simple as that.' As I said earlier, sometimes you have to make your own decisions. Live by the sword, die by the sword.

At the time of writing, Andre has just joined Birmingham City on loan. Tony Mowbray, 'Mogga', who had always asked me 'why didn't he come to Blackburn?' whenever I bumped into him, had finally got his man. Andre's buzzing off that wanted feeling, just as I did off that 'got you at last' comment from John Lyall. A little bit of love goes a long way, let me tell you.

It seems like only yesterday when Andre scored on his debut, but he's 24 now. I'm trying to tell him how quick it goes. Six years will go by in a blink of an eye and he'll be 30. Might he end up back at Ipswich one day? Who knows? I'd love that, obviously, but the stars would have to align. I think, ultimately, he might end up abroad. The style could suit him. I had the chance to play in Europe later in my career, but didn't feel equipped to do so. That's a shame because I've seen the life experiences that Dion has got from living in the US.

My third son, Emile, was born in 2005 after I'd retired. My wife and I had split up at that time, but I went back and tried to rebuild our relationship. That didn't work, but we did get something special out of it. Emile's just turned 18 and is a cheeky one. The youngest always are. At the moment he's with me, playing in the Ipswich Town Foundation, and is doing really well. He was a slow-burner with his football, he didn't really know what it took to make it, but he's getting there now, bit by bit, and is showing a lot of talent. Like his brothers, he's just a great kid. He does get picked on by all of us, but he's got the personality to handle it and give it back. He makes me laugh, which I need. His banter is very sharp.

Have I been a good dad? You'd have to ask them. All I know is that I'm there for them and would do anything for them.

I'm actually in awe of my three boys. They're incredible people and I couldn't be prouder of the men they've grown up to become. When I feel down, I should think about them. That should get me over it. Sometimes it does.

20

Just Handcuff Me Please

I WAS blagging it for a long time. Emotions were buried deep and not surfacing. That was always going to have consequences at some point. Things finally came to a head in 2019.

There were various triggers. The first, as touched upon, was that I was just not stimulated. Coaching was never enough. I missed the everyday action of a changing room environment.

I was living in a flat on my own down by the docks when my old girlfriend, Cathy, suggested we try again. I gave up my place and moved back in with her but after a day or so I could feel it just wasn't right. I shouldn't have gone back. I think I just liked the thought of it.

As I said before, something always stopped me from feeling comfortable when things were just nice. When everything is going all right there's this voice that tells you to mess things up to feel normal again. It's weird. I don't know if you'll understand that or not. Most people get used to that flat line, normal life, whereas my life has constantly been up and down, always from the top of the mountain to the bottom of the ocean. That becomes your norm.

I'm still good friends with Cathy now. She had a son who was six when I first met her. I wasn't his father, but I tried to be a male role model for him. Still today, if he ever needs anything I'm there. It's like that. Me not being able to conquer that demon of 'this is the good life, don't mess it up' was what did for us. After all the hassle I gave her, she was still really good to me when I was in trouble further down the line. I'm thankful for that.

After quickly deciding I was better on my own, I tried to get my old flat back. But it had already gone, so I had to go and live with Andre. I was uncomfortable about that because I knew he hadn't moved out of his mum's to end up living with me. We got on, but I was very conscious of not outstaying my welcome.

I just felt lost. I was struggling to get out of bed at times. I was having panic attacks, though I didn't know it was that at the time because I'd never had them before. I'd been down before, we all get down, but this was something different. I was just constantly on edge, always ready to have an argument and cause a commotion. I'd point at people and say, 'I'm not too sure on him.' I know now that was my own insecurities.

Still, I ignored it because I'd grown up in an old-school football environment where it was seen as a weakness to admit to any problems.

Everything was suffocating me. The town. Everybody. Eventually I hit a brick wall. You can only take so much before you hit that point. Some people kill themselves. With me it was self-destructive behaviour.

In March, with Andre struggling for game time, I went on a bus to West Brom with a group known as the 'Ipswich Punishment Squad'. I wouldn't say they were hooligans, but they could look after themselves, put it that way. I knew a couple of them. 'Come with us,' they said. Like always, I couldn't say no. Like always, I was chasing a cheap thrill. They loved me and I loved that. We went to the pub, got steamed up and then moved on to the match. It was a great laugh and a brief escape from my own head. Subconsciously was I trying to reconnect with the excitement of my days in the North Stand? I don't know, but I shouldn't have been putting myself in that position. *I wish it didn't happen, but it did.* I felt I was no better than that. I was dipping.

Soon enough, the season came to an end. That was when I was really in trouble. The summer has always been a fragile time for me. When the football stops, I'm on my own. I've always struggled most when I'm on my own. I had a period where I wasn't working. My coaching role at the Ipswich academy had finished for the season, my coaching job at Broke Hall Primary School was about to stop for the holidays and I started having loads of time on my hands.

It was around that same time an offer came in for Andre – from Norwich City. After some negotiations, Ipswich agreed a fee of £3.4m. Now it was up to him if he wanted to go. *Fucking hell.*

We're all in this room – me, him, his agent, Norwich representatives. Ipswich are in League One, Norwich are in the Prem. 'This is a great move!' they're all telling him. Andre's listening. He's not got that same deep-rooted Ipswich background that I've got. He's ambitious, makes his own decisions and wants his career to go further.

I just had to go along with it as a supportive dad. Obviously, I'll follow him and back him all the way wherever he goes, but inside I was worried. My mind was racing. I was thinking things like, 'That's my status in Ipswich gone for ever,' and, 'I've got to go to Carrow Road, where am I going to sit? I'm going to get beat up,' and, 'If you don't absolutely smash it from day one, you'll be hated there.'

What didn't help was that those talks dragged on for ages. I think Norwich were waiting on some sales to happen before they could progress with it.

That situation proved a tipping point for my mental health. It added another layer of emotion on top of the guilt I felt about my ex-wife and general restlessness I had with life. I thought I was a bad person and I didn't want to be a bad person. Instead of getting to the root cause of those feelings, this Norwich thing gave me the easy 'out' of being angry with the world. I'd always find a way to pin the blame on others for my actions.

Stupid things started to happen. Several times I drove into the back of somebody when not concentrating. I'd be just crawling along and then – bang! Completely sober, but my mind had gone. I'd get out of the car, see there wasn't too much damage, say sorry and be on my way. The worst one was when I went into the back of a bus. The bus driver got out and I just stayed sat in the car staring into space. I watched him inspect the back of his bus, he nodded as if to say 'that's all right', I mouthed to him 'how's my car?' and he gave me a thumbs up. Off we went. I drove around the corner, pulled over, got out and took a look. The front of my car was completely caved in. I didn't even care.

My coping mechanism was to be stone-faced, isolate and shut off. When alone my mind raced. Suicidal thoughts? No. Never. It was more stupid thoughts like 'I'm going to kill someone'. I'd invent scenarios in my head where someone did something bad to my kids and I'd think about what I was going to do to them.

Those thoughts weren't pretty. They were horrible. There was no need for me to think like that, either. It was based on nothing whatsoever. It was just made-up drama in my head. I was never going to do anything like that, I've never been a fighter or a horrible person, but that's where my mind was going. That was just my way of not thinking about me. That's where I was.

I'd tell myself, 'Stop! Pull yourself out of it!' I would pull myself out of it, then two weeks later I'd be back in those thoughts again. You could have put an egg on my brain and fried it. Thoughts were constantly sizzling.

I'm not a mental health expert, and I've not really been diagnosed, so I can't tell you what it was exactly. All I know is my body was telling me there was a problem. I'd be lying down, just watching the telly, and I could feel my heart racing in my chest for no reason. *Du-du, du-du, du-du.* I'd want it to stop, but it wouldn't go away. I couldn't sleep. I'd try to open a bottle and it would be shaking all over the place. But I wasn't facing it. I wasn't looking at it correctly. I wasn't thinking about it from a mental health perspective.

I was just thinking, 'Maybe my partying is catching up with me?'

So what did I do? The most illogical thing. I turned to cocaine. People might think I was trying to chase the buzz from my football career. No, no, no. I was struggling. Sober was horrific. The stress and anxiety was through the roof. Bad thoughts. This was not a buzz. This was, 'I need to take this away.' It worked too. The drugs did take it away – that's the sad thing about it. Cocaine stopped me just sitting there doing nothing. It made me get out of bed and do things. It killed time and made my day go quicker. I wouldn't get completely wired, but I'd take enough to stop that paralysis and occupy my mind.

I need to be clear here that during my football career I only took drugs during the summer. Post football it had only been once in a blue moon. I'd only do it when I went out. I'd never have it in the house. Never. I've always been able to function. I've got three kids, I have to. I'm not an addict who's craving drink or drugs all the time. It's not like that.

But increasingly, if there were weeks where I didn't have much on, I would turn to them. I simply couldn't handle the days when I was not doing anything. If I had something to do all day, then I wouldn't think about the drugs. But in those quiet moments I can't relax, I can't switch off. I need that stimulation. I've got to fill the gaps. Too much time on my hands has always been my biggest problem. That's when the drugs came in.

The scary thing about it is that I didn't even have to pay for them. Why? I don't know. It was just, 'Anytime you need it, just ring this number and someone will drop it off.' No questions asked. That's my entitled mindset again. I'm not proud of that. It is what it is.

Things had been bubbling under for a long time and now they were bubbling over. I knew something bad was about to happen, I just didn't know what or when. I could just feel myself going to lower ground.

This one particular day was worse than usual. My edginess started early. I went to the guy's house who had the drugs and was there all day. I could have stayed there, but I sort of sobered up. I sat in my car outside, thought about sleeping there, and then decided, stupidly, to try and get home. I got all the way through town and when I reached Foxhall Road post office I thought, 'Phew, I've done it.' Two seconds later I saw blue lights in my rear-view mirror.

When they pulled me over the police said, 'We don't want you for drink, we want you for drugs.' Someone had obviously rung it in. Was it someone who had been listening in on conversations I'd had down the pub? Was it someone I knew? Back then, that added to my paranoia. Now I've got more perspective. You can't control what other people do, but you can control what you do. I only had myself to blame.

As the police arrested me, I barely said a word. I just surrendered, no fuss. It was like, 'Just handcuff me please, put me in the car and do what you need to do.' Looking back, did I want to get caught? I sometimes wonder. Maybe I did. I can't say that was definitely the case, but it might have been because you only put yourself in a situation like that if something's not right. If you can't talk to somebody about how you're feeling, are you going to take extreme measures to get it out there?

They took me to the station and did the tests. They found 800ug (0.8mg) of benzoylecgonine, a compound found in cocaine, in my bloodstream. That put me 16 times above the 'accidental exposure' limit. It's not a good story. *I wish it didn't happen, but it did happen.*

The hardest bit was having to tell Andre the next morning. I was in a right state. 'Right, calm down, I get it,' he told me. 'Thank you, son.'

The great thing about all my kids is that they have never, ever judged me. I've shown them more emotion than I have anyone else. If I didn't do that, they wouldn't understand what was going on, they'd think I'm a bad person, but they knew something was bubbling over because I was having breakdowns in front of them, crying. After all the personal embarrassment I've brought them, they've never wavered in their support. I'll always be grateful for that.

The next people I had to tell were my employers at Broke Hall School. I'd been there for seven years, coaching two times a week. That job was never about money. You know when you are loved at certain places and the kids there absolutely adored me. When I had to go in and tell those children that I wasn't going to be there for a while, possibly ever, that was really difficult.

Next on the confession list was Ipswich Town. I arranged a meeting at Trongs, a Chinese restaurant on St Nicholas Street, with a club representative. I got straight to the point – 'I've fucked up.' I told them what had happened and braced myself for an instant sacking, major bollocking or, at the very least, a very disappointed look.

'That's all right! We've all made mistakes!' came the cheery response. I was not expecting that reaction.

'By the way, we want Andre to sign a new contract.'

'OK – but what about what I've just told you?'

'Don't worry about that! We're going to offer you a full-time job and a car.'

I'd gone there with my tail between my legs and come out with the offer of a full-time job and a car. You can't make this up! That really messed with my head.

The trouble was that Andre's agent now thought I'd gone behind his back to get Andre to stay at Ipswich. Things got lost in translation. Me and Andre had a tiny little falling-out because he thought I arranged that meeting to talk about his contract. That was a strange time.

I think that story shows you what the football industry is like. I didn't need qualifications to be a coach when Andre was at the club. I could do whatever I wanted when Andre was there. I was unsackable when Andre was there. As soon as he left for QPR in 2021 though it was, 'Sorry Jason, you haven't got your badges, there's not a role for you in the academy any more.'

The wait for the court case was only supposed to be three weeks, but it ended up taking six months. The longer it went on the worse I was getting. I couldn't handle it. My drug-taking went into overdrive. I just lost the plot. That period was when I was at my lowest. I went into a black hole that I wouldn't wish on anybody.

Over those few months, I kept getting pulled by the police. The first time was when I was taking Andre, who was injured at the time, into the training ground. I was waiting to come out of Brookhill Way, at the T-junction, and a police car went by. He'd obviously seen me out the corner of his eye and stopped. I pulled out, went past him and the blue lights came on. 'It's just a random stop to check your details. Yeah, you're all right, on your way.' They didn't breathalyse me or drug-test me, they were just making a nuisance of themselves really.

Another time, Andre was driving and I was in the passenger seat. We were coming down past the hospital, the police came by on the outside, pulled in front of us and I joked to Andre, 'You've got me in the car mate, you're going to get a pull!' Sure enough, we turned right on to Foxhall Road, got down by Copleston School, his old school of all places, and he pulled us. Again, apparently just a random check.

This went on and on. Eight times in total I got stopped – six times when I was driving, twice when I was a passenger with Andre. It was obvious they were just going to keep pulling me no matter what.

I've got a lot of time for the police. I respect the police. I know some police people and they're good people. But you always get some arseholes in every industry. Repeatedly stopping someone while they wait for a court case – is that allowed? I don't know. I guess I was fair game after what I'd done. I get it, in a way, but it felt too much. And stopping us when Andre's driving, what's that all about? Maybe they saw me and that was the reason. Or maybe they just saw a young black boy wearing a baseball cap driving a nice Mercedes and thought, 'How's he got that car?' I don't know.

I sold my car after all that and I've not driven since. It's traumatising getting pulled over by the police. Every time I see blue lights now I panic. It's a horrible feeling. Hopefully I'll get my confidence back at some point.

Everything was colliding at that time. I was just frustrated with life. Everything I'd tried to fight had come to a head. Everything I'd bottled up had created this. I was thinking there was no way back. *I'm finished. Where can I run, where can I hide?*

Ipswich was suffocating me. I love my town, but everybody knows me. For some reason, I don't know why, it has got worse over the years. Everybody will say hello. I have to pretend I know people because I don't want to come across as rude. I needed to get out, but where could I go? I couldn't figure it out. The US was on my mind. I thought about it, but I knew I couldn't leave the boys and my mum. Ipswich has been my life. Although I've threatened to leave a few times, I never could.

Apart from my sons, no one knew where my head was at. People looking in from the outside probably thought I was all right. Sometimes it's all an act, isn't it? Everybody wears a mask.

The one person who saw through it was my old team-mate, Simon Milton. I'd see him out and about and he'd ask, 'Are you all right?' and I'd reply, 'Yeah, I'm fine.' Most people accept that answer and walk off. Milts knew something wasn't right, though, and gently kept digging. He was the first one where I thought, 'Uh oh, he can read me like a book.'

That was three weeks before the court case. He asked me to go for lunch and I couldn't think of an excuse to get out of it. I went to Milsoms not planning to say anything, but it all ended up coming out. I remember it so well. He was listening, just shaking his head as the floodgates opened. I'd stop talking, he'd just say 'OK', then I'd go 'there's more!' and carry on.

The great thing about Milts is that he gets things done. By the next day I had the PFA and various people ringing me up offering me services. I knew those services were available to me, but I would never have reached out to them on my own.

Milts also got in touch with the *East Anglian Daily Times* and *Ipswich Star* to arrange an interview that would be published on the day of the court ruling. I went into their offices on Portman Road and was relieved that they sent out Ipswich Town reporter Stuart Watson, someone I knew through his coverage of Andre's journey. I told Stuart, who has subsequently helped me write this book, what had been going on.

Don't get me wrong, getting my suit on and going into Ipswich Magistrates' Court, not knowing what the outcome was going to be, was a horrible feeling. The biggest emotion I had that day was one of relief. It was like a pressure valve had been released.

There are a few people I need to thank here. Horry Money, a solicitor and big Town fan, helped me on the legal side of things, while Milts and Lee O'Neill, who was the club's general manager of football operations at that time, both stood up and gave me character references in court. I have to say, Ipswich

Town were fantastic for me. I know I've talked cynically about Andre being a factor in that, and I do think that was the case, but the club did give me a new job three years down the line, in the charitable arm known as the Ipswich Town Foundation, and that has been massive for my mental health. They didn't have to give me a second chance, but they did. I really appreciate my club sticking by me like that.

On a personal level, long-time friends Dennis Tennial and Pasquale Iachetta were big players for me at that time. Obviously, my family rallied around too. I'm so thankful for their support. I should have opened up to them sooner.

The verdict came through. I was banned from driving for 14 months, fined £440 plus £105 costs and a £32 victim surcharge. The next morning my interview was at the top of the websites and took up the first few pages of the papers. I didn't know what sort of response I was going to get. To be honest, I didn't really care. Just speaking had felt like a huge weight off my shoulders.

The reaction was overwhelming. Loads of people quite close to me were reaching out saying, 'Yeah man, I've been through the same.' Someone I knew told me they'd recently tried to kill themselves. I'd never have thought that about them. It just shows, you never really know what's going on in other people's lives.

If I hadn't done that story then people wouldn't have perceived me the way they did. They'd have just seen 'drug driver' and cast their judgement. Rightly so. People can only judge you on what you show them. That's been a big lesson for me.

When Milts got to me I was a mess. If that lunch hadn't happened then this might have been a different story. I'll never forget what he did for me at that moment. If he hadn't set things in motion then the consequences could have been huge.

As I'm piecing everything together and trying to join the dots, I've thought about where certain people were when I've been in trouble. The people who came through for me after that article really surprised me. The people I thought would be there weren't there.

For me, being a friend is going out of your comfort zone for someone in their times of trouble, not just being there when I'm doing well in my career and have money. A true friend does something monstrous for you. They will always say what you don't want to hear, which I probably needed earlier in my life. No one ever said to me, 'Jason, stop, what are you doing?' I needed someone to ring me up after a game, talk to me about how it had gone and say, 'Don't go too mad tonight, I'll be ringing you at 11 o'clock tomorrow.'

My wife tried all that, but there was a disconnect in my brain. I would think 'she's just nagging again'. The other voices in my life, wrongly, drowned her out. I've always been 'live for today'. I've always been that guy. Would I have listened more to a father figure? I'll never know.

The drug-drive story is not a good one. It's not something I'm proud of at all. But something bad had to happen to me in order to be this man today. Now things are starting to become clearer for me, I feel I can start talking about it. I wouldn't have been able to a couple of years ago.

21

It's Good to Talk

THE SINGLE most horrible thing in the world has to be the death of one of your children. My sister Carolyn – and I still can't believe I'm saying this – lost two of her boys in the space of two years.

My nephew John was 12 years younger than me, but we were very close as he grew up. He was a staunch Ipswich fan and would always go to the games with a 'Dozzell' shirt on. Even when I stopped playing, he'd still wear that shirt.

John was always a bundle of laughs. He was the joker in the room. He was just a funny, funny guy. In his later years he moved to Eindhoven, met a Dutch girl, they had twins – a boy and a girl – and he lived his life.

'Maybe it was fate that he ended up over there,' says Carolyn, when we sat down to properly discuss the tragic events of the last few years for the very first time.

'The first football shirt I bought John as a nine-year-old boy was a Holland one with Ruud Gullit's name on the back. Ipswich Town have had this great affinity with Dutch football, haven't they? I don't know.'

It was August 2020, just as Covid lockdown rules were being eased and Rishi Sunak was encouraging everyone to 'eat out, to help out', that the devastating news came through. John, the eldest of Carolyn's five children at 40 years old, had fallen down the stairs and hit his head. Heartbreakingly, it was his daughter, who was ten at the time, who found him there when she woke up in the morning.

'I thank God that myself and his father, plus his brothers and sisters, were able to go out there, because I know there were a lot of people who lost loved ones during Covid who weren't able to do that, including my youngest daughter who lives in Cape Town,' says Carolyn.

'We got to the hospital and discovered he had a bleed on the brain. He was on the machines. We talked to him, but I don't think he knew we were there.

'We went back to a hotel, but about an hour later his wife called us and said, "I think you better come back." The doctors pulled me to one side and said they couldn't do anything more. I'm just very grateful that he didn't suffer.

'Thankfully we were all able to go back out for the funeral and say goodbye. That was very much done in John's style. There was a playlist of his favourite music. He had a plain pine coffin and everybody put their handprints on it in different colours, writing little messages. It was a real celebration of his life. Then we came home and tried to process what had happened.'

As I said before, John and I were close growing up. My nephew was gone, but I wasn't able to say goodbye. That's because only a few people could go over to the funeral due to

Covid. The extended family had to watch it via Zoom. It was heart-wrenching. Really sad.

Then, less than two years later, the unimaginable happened. Carolyn received a knock on the door out of the blue. It was the police informing her that her other son had taken his own life.

Tom was 39 years old. When they found him, the only things he had on him were his car keys and a picture of John. He was grieving his older brother and I think other things in his life weren't going to plan. It all came to a head.

It was a 45-minute drive to the place where he did what he did. I can't stop thinking about that. What is so bad that you've made your decision not to turn back? I just wish he'd reached out and made contact with somebody.

Again, this is mental health. People don't understand it. I don't understand it. It's clearer to me now, but maybe it wasn't clear to Tom if he saw that as his only option.

'I don't think we were aware of just how bad Tom's mental health was,' says Carolyn. 'We knew he had his struggles, but the persona he presented outwardly was something different.

'Tom did get some support from different services. He had so many sessions and, according to him, they said he was on the right track. He seemed to be OK, but then, and I only found this out afterwards, he dipped and couldn't really get access to the services again.

'You hear people say, "If I'd have known, I could have stopped it." I'm not sure you can. How dark a place are you in to think that's your only option? I do take something from knowing he's at peace now.

'I was left in a state of shock. It wasn't thinking, "Why has this happened to me?" It was more like, "How can somebody lose one child and then another so quickly after?" It was just unreal.

'We were out of Covid by then but still wearing masks. The whole experience of grief was very, very different this time. With John it was very calm. Maybe it's just the way they do things in Holland, but John passed on the Monday and by the Friday they had his service. With Tom it was nearly six weeks before we could have the funeral because they obviously have to investigate when someone takes their own life. That was a really, really difficult period.'

What happened to my sister is just so unfair. I will never be able to fully understand what she's been through and is still going through. I do not for one minute underestimate how hard it must have been for her to speak so openly about it all like this. I'm so proud of her for doing so.

Tom's death made me reflect on my own state of mind back in 2019. I had given up. Three weeks before that court case I was thinking 'there's no way out of this'. I wasn't seeking help or reaching out. I'd shut down. If that lunch with Milts hadn't happened then who knows how things would have played out? Suicide never crossed my mind, but what happened to Tom did make me wonder if I might have reached that point. Me staring the abyss in the face was the drug-driving incident. What if I hadn't been caught that night, though?

Mental health to me, back then, was somebody being 'nuts'. I'm ashamed to say that now, but naively that's how I viewed it. Now I know mental health takes on all different forms. It can be anxiety. It can be depression. It can be an inability to get up in the mornings. It can be a lot of different things.

You hate yourself. You think you're the only one who's got it. I thought I was mental. I wasn't mental. I just had bad mental health. If your heart's pumping too fast, if you're edgy, that's all part of it. But I didn't think it was. I thought it was just 'one of those days'.

I'd accumulated a hell of a lot of mental baggage by the time I got to 2019 because I can take a lot. I always have been able to soak stuff up. But everyone has their breaking point.

All I know is that mental health is a fucker – especially, it seems, with men of a certain age group.

More than 6,000 people across the UK and Republic of Ireland take their own lives each year. The Office for National Statistics shows men make up 75 per cent of that number, with those aged between 40 and 55 most at risk.

According to the Samaritans, only a third of people who die by suicide have been in contact with specialist mental health services in the year before their death.

Yes, it's immensely difficult to talk about, but this cannot remain a taboo topic. Are we doing enough as a society to let people know it's OK not to be OK? Are there enough mental health services in place for those who can be encouraged to reach out? In this digital world of texting and social media, do we all need to stop showing off online and put more of an effort into properly and truthfully connecting with our friends in person?

Tom was completely different to John. He kept himself to himself and was quite guarded. It must have been a build-up over a long period of time of him not talking about anything, probably like it was a build-up over years for me.

You can pretend, both to yourself and others, that you're fine. You can fake it – and that's dangerous. It came to a head for me, not in the way it did with Tom, but it did come to a head. Something eventually has to give.

As someone who has been in that dark hole, I know how easy it is to withdraw and put on a mask when you need to. No one around me would have known how bad things were. No one knew, really, how bad things were with Tom.

Carolyn explained, 'Tom was out the night before and, apparently, he'd asked a friend to take a picture of him, insisting it had to be from the waist up. I think the friend took a few pictures and Tom wasn't happy until he'd got the exact one he wanted. When that friend told me that story it didn't initially mean anything to me, but then I remembered that the picture used at John's funeral was very similar – from the waist up. I think Tom wanted a similar picture.

'The other day I zoomed in on the picture of John's coffin to read some of those messages and the one from Tom said something like "can't wait 'til we meet again". Did that mean something? I don't know. I can't speak for someone who isn't here, but did that make things easier for him? Did he think somebody was waiting for him when he left this world?

'People always say, "You don't think about your children going before you," and they're right. You absolutely don't. You try to move on with life, life does go on, but you have your difficult days – obvious moments like the day of their passing, birthdays, Father's Day, Mother's Day. Things like that really do get to me. Other days I'm fine. I have days where I think, it's time to try and be happy again. No matter how hard you try though it's really, really difficult.

'Now I react differently when I hear about young people dying. There was that young boy stabbed in Ipswich town centre recently. Before my reaction would have been, "That's an awful thing to happen, what's the world coming to?" Now I instantly think, "Oh my God, a mother's lost her child." There's an absolutely different perspective. Now I know how that feels.

'You don't stop thinking about them. I think about death very differently now knowing that two of my children are somewhere else. Whenever and wherever I go, I know they'll be there.'

Tom's passing catapulted mental health more into my head and made me think about the power of talking. After I did that story in the newspaper opening up about my struggles, I couldn't believe the letters I received. There was no contact like that from any footballers, though. They're a funny breed. There's still that stigma in our industry, I think. You can't be vulnerable because it's seen as a sign of weakness. I know there are ex-footballers like me going around with no direction. But they're not going to reach out. I know they're not. Not the old-school players, anyway. That must change.

I do think that's changing for the younger generation. A boy I'm coaching called me one day saying, 'I want to speak to you.' We met up, along with another coach, and he told us he'd tried to kill himself. I was not expecting that. He's the best player on the pitch and the bubbliest in the changing room. I thought the people who were struggling would be quiet and wouldn't exert themselves. He was the opposite. It just shows, you don't know what's going on in anyone's head.

Look at Gary Speed. In the morning, he was on *Football Focus*, then in the afternoon he took his own life. Robin Williams – a comedian, someone who makes people laugh – committed suicide. It just shows you that people can mask their pain, they can hide it from you. It doesn't discriminate. No one is immune from it. Don't underestimate anyone's mental health, because we can all pretend we're fine.

I know now that people want to help me. I know now that people will give you a second chance. Back then I didn't. My thought process was 'don't be a burden'.

If I hadn't done that newspaper article then I wouldn't have written this book. And if I hadn't written this book then I wouldn't have had the greater understanding of myself that I now have. Everything's a bit clearer now. I can recognise the warning signs. Your brain can tell you one thing, but your body can tell you another. If I feel a bit edgy the first person I reach out to is Simon Milton.

'I don't talk about it like this very often at all,' admitted Carolyn. 'I see people who I haven't seen since it happened and they say, "I'm sorry for your loss." I thank them, but that's it. I don't share my emotions. Not at all. I think that's been us as a family. We don't necessarily speak like that.'

She's right. As a family we've never dug too deep. There's a lot to talk about, but there also isn't because we've got no information to go on. I think that's something we've inherited. It comes from the top. Mum doesn't really open up and we've probably continued that. There's a pattern. I would imagine a lot of people in our family keep a lot locked up inside. That's not healthy.

For the first time in our lives, Carolyn and I touched upon the subject of her, Kenny, Tony, Cheryl and Nathan being put into care, while myself and Tootie stayed with Mum. Tootie and I eventually tracked down our father, but the others didn't entertain the idea.

'None of us asked some of the questions that we perhaps wanted answers to,' she admits. 'Then I think you get to an age where you think "it's too late" and "would it make a difference?" Is it? Would it? I don't know.'

I asked Carolyn if she'd ever had a conversation with mum about her upbringing and father. 'No,' was the reply. Like me, her instinct was to 'protect' emotions. It gets us back on to the subject of Tom's passing.

'My other children, my brothers and sisters, yourself included Jason, our mum – you were all grieving in your own ways,' she says. 'There were times where I felt I had to be strong to support them – certainly my own children. If I break down, what good is it to them?

'I have my moments when I'm alone and in my own space. I don't show it to others. That's not because I can't show it, because I can, but I don't want other people to be sad because I'm sad.'

Is it healthy for parents to hide that vulnerability from their children, though? If you try to stay strong then people think you're all right when you're not. If my boys don't know where my head's at then they can't help me. And if I'm not in a good place, I can't help them.

As I've said, there's been three or four times I've broken down in front of my boys. I haven't done that with anyone else, but I've had to show them. They need to know where I'm at. Because I've been so open with them, they have never judged me. I've learned that if you say "look, I'm in trouble", people will look after you. But if you don't reach out, you're invisible.

'There's that saying of "people will help you if you want to help yourself",' said Carolyn, when we discussed the above. Very true. So how can you help someone to want to help themselves? I think a big thing is making them realise they are not the only one. We all think we're the only one struggling, but we're really not.

It's good to talk. It's OK not to be OK. You're not going to feel like this for ever. Just take each day as it comes. We need to keep having those conversations. If I can help anybody by using the small platform I've got, then I will. I have to.

22

Trying Not to Judge

THE ALARMS at Warren Hill prison suddenly pierced the air. I looked up and saw an air ambulance circling overhead.

Screws were running all over the place shouting commands. 'Everyone back into your rooms!' One of them caught my panicked eye, pointed and said, 'Get in there.' I scurried into the gym and the door was quickly shut behind me. Then came the click of the lock.

I looked at my watch – it was four o'clock. I went up to the little gate on the door and got the attention of the prison officer on the other side. 'Can you let me out, mate?' 'You ain't going anywhere, pal,' he replied. 'There's been a stabbing, no one's leaving.'

After what felt like an age, I heard a crackly voice come through on that guy's walkie-talkie. 'Count one finished, count two commencing. Over.' *Please, no.* I was starting to not feel good. I'm not in charge of this. I'm feeling anxious, claustrophobic. I want to go. This is not good for my mental health.

I went up to the guy guarding the door again, pleading this time. 'Mate, please, my girlfriend's waiting for me outside, just let me out!' I instantly regretted saying that. 'Shut up you idiot, I've told you, you're not getting out.'

Three hours I was held in that gym. I was virtually climbing the walls. I found out later that the victim had been stabbed three times – once in the abdomen and twice in the neck. I still don't know if he survived or not.

* * *

The Twinning Project's objective is a simple one: to pair all 117 prisons across England and Wales with a local professional football club.

Staff from those clubs then go into those prisons to deliver once-a-week coaching courses to a select few prisoners who are close to serving their time inside. At the end of the six-week block they get an FA-accredited Level One Sports Leadership qualification.

The idea is that those football sessions boost the mental and physical health of the prisoner and improve their life chances upon release. Giving them purpose and value, a platform for meaningful social relationships, as well as improved employment chances will, research has shown, drastically reduce their likelihood of reoffending.

Ipswich Town is twinned with two prisons in Suffolk. Warren Hill is a 'Category C' prison located in the small peninsula village of Hollesley just south of Woodbridge. Less than a mile down the road is Hollesley Bay. Classed as 'Category D', it has minimal security and allows eligible risk-assessed inmates to spend most of their day away from the prison on licence to carry out work or education.

When I was asked, as part of my work with the Ipswich Town Foundation, to get involved in the project I was a bit wary to begin with. My brother Tony has done a fair bit of time. He was in and out of jail sporadically, always for football violence, doing several years in places like Wayland in Norwich and Highpoint in Newmarket. I visited him every week when I could.

Tony had to fight to fit in when it came to real life and I'm sure he had to fight to fit in when it came to prisons. Whenever I sat down to speak with him in the canteen, he was never going to be one to admit, 'It's hard in here, I'm struggling.' I could just tell, however, that life inside wasn't pretty.

With that in mind, I thought, 'I'm going to be badly out of my comfort zone here,' but in the end I said I'd give it a go. I felt in a better place mentally. I wanted to challenge myself and help others.

I'll never forget my first visit to Hollesley Bay. As soon as I got out of the car this guy came rushing towards me at speed outside the front entrance. I took a couple of steps back in instinctive fear. *What have I got myself into here?* Then he suddenly skidded to a stop and said all excitedly, 'All right mate, can you get me a QPR shirt?' A wave of relief flooded through my body. 'Yeah, yeah, no worries mate, will do.' That got the heart rate going, I can tell you!

I was so nervous as I made my way into the building to face some hardened criminals. *Was this a good idea? How are they going to take me?* Then I got inside and straight away there were shouts of, 'Jason! Jason! You know my dad. Do you remember this?' And, 'Jason, I know your brother!' My colleague from the ITFC Foundation, Andy, was looking at me in disbelief. I could tell he was thinking, 'What on earth is going on here?!' That reception eased some of the fears.

My job that day was to deliver a coaching course, but I'd gone there with different motivations. Following the court case, the newspaper article, my nephews dying and that hug with my dad I'd been doing a lot of thinking. On the way to that prison I told myself, 'I'm going to get these guys to talk.'

I couldn't just go in there as an ex-Premier League footballer and expect them to open up, though. It doesn't work like that. I knew I had to give them something to get something back. So, when we sat down in the classroom, I spoke to them openly about my life. I tried to tell them things about me that might resonate a little bit. No father, no guidance – I think that struck a chord with quite a few. I told them about my mental health issues after football.

I also told them about how Tony had dealt with coming in and out of prison and how everybody is one bad decision or mad moment away from being in jail. I acknowledged that I could have knocked someone over driving under the influence and how it could easily be me in there with them. If I'd grown up the way I did in London rather than Ipswich then I could have ended up being drawn into trouble. Who knows?

I never asked them about what they'd done and where their heads were at, but at the end of the session they all came over one-by-one and told me their stories. For a complete stranger to feel they'd got the green light to tell me, 'I was an armed robber, I shot people', was quite something. It made me feel good.

The next six-week block was at Warren Hill. I went there feeling under pressure because some of these guys had served 25-plus years. I knew some of them were going to be big, big criminals, people who have committed murder. It can be quite unnerving when you're in the same room as people like that and I knew they'd sense that.

You have to walk through the gym to get to the classroom at Warren Hill. My God, I haven't seen bodies like that before. There were muscles coming out of muscles. They must just be pumping iron all day. It was a case of keeping my head down and trying not to make eye contact before someone said something. But again, taking the same approach as before, I managed to get them all to talk. That was a real buzz.

There was, however, one moment on that first day at Warren Hill that made me stop in my tracks. I was out on the pitch coaching, watching this boy who's got a beautiful left foot. I said to him, 'You used to play, didn't you?' I wish I'd never asked. He told me he'd been released by Stoke City and that triggered something in my brain. As soon as I got back to the car, I Googled him and this story from 2012 came up.

'An ex-Premier League football academy player, jailed in September for killing his girlfriend, has had his sentence increased by five years. Andrew Hall, 18, released by Stoke City in May, pleaded guilty to murdering Megan-Leigh Peat, 15, at a house in Ampthill, Bedfordshire, on 9 June. Megan, described by family as a caring, loving and bright girl, suffered at least 60 stab wounds in the attack. Hall was jailed for life with a minimum term of ten years, but this has been increased to 15 by the Court of Appeal.'

That really put a knot in my stomach. *What am I dealing with here? Can I be around people like this for my own mental state?* It really got me thinking.

These people are the leftovers in society, the last leaves in the pile. Do you just let them rot? When you stop and think about what some of them have done it can be very easy to come to that conclusion. Then I think that some of them are only 35 and they've been in there 18 years – kids when they went in, grown men now. Would you want to be judged on how you were at 17 or 18?

In the end, I decided it's not my role to judge. Ipswich Town have sent me, just do your job. Simple as that.

I do also recognise that these are hard people to read. My issues are pretty easy to work out compared to theirs. These are hardened criminals who can play nice on the surface but potentially be downright nasty underneath. That's what can make it confusing. They can be lovely to me, but there has to be a switch still in there with some of them.

Ultimately though, as I say, I can only judge them on what they show me. And what they show me is that they have remorse for their past and want to change for the better. Who knows if that's going to be the case when they get out, no one can say that for certain, but I do believe everyone deserves a second chance. I do believe in rehabilitation. As the Twinning Project motto goes, 'We all make mistakes. Don't let that be a reason to give up on somebody.' I know I've certainly made mistakes. I'm pretty sure you have too at some stage.

I've done a few of the six-week coaching blocks at the two prisons now and it's always a proud moment when I see the guys come to Portman Road for graduation day. I'd like to think I've helped them in a little way without them all necessarily knowing it.

I invited Stuart, who helped me write this book, along to one of those final sessions to get a feel for what it's all about. Unbeknownst to me he took one of the guys, Gordon, off for a quiet chat.

Asked for a contribution to this book, Gordon said, 'For some context, I have supported Ipswich since I was five, was born the same year as Jason and watched him growing up.

'Then, a few years ago, I went to a Milton Keynes away game, we pulled up in the car park and, as I got out, I saw him. I was saying to my kids, "That's Jason Dozzell!" and he looked over and smiled.

'My kids were in awe of him. "Oh my God, it's Jason Dozzell!" He was two cars away and I beckoned him over. He smiled. "Hello mate!" We were laughing and chatting. He was 100 per cent approachable. He was just so good with my kids. He was putting his arm around them, telling them football stories and giving them advice. To watch my kids so at ease with a famous footballer like that was amazing. When we got to the game, he asked them, "Where are you standing? Because I'm standing with you and your dad." We watched the game together.'

Gordon, I'm told, paused at this point of the conversation to wipe a solitary tear from his eye.

'Unfortunately, further down the line, I've found myself in the position where I'm at Her Majesty's Pleasure, or rather His Majesty's Pleasure now.

'When I said to my kids that I'd got on the Ipswich Town training academy with Twinnings they couldn't believe it. Sorry, I'm trying not to get upset here because I love my kids to bits and I miss them.

'Then I turned up for the first session, Jason saw me and said, "What on earth are you doing in here?!" I thought exactly the same! I told him, "Listen mate, I'll tell you another time."

'I phoned my kids straight away afterwards and said, "I've started that Ipswich Town thing and you'll never guess who was there – Jason Dozzell." "No way!" "Yeah, and he remembered me from Milton Keynes." I was crying on the phone.

'The next week I told Jason about that conversation with my kids and he took me to one side, away from the other lads, gave me a hug and said, "When you're out of jail we're going to catch up." He's just a nice guy. He doesn't have that celebrity air about him. He's just a normal geezer. To me, he's a man's man.

'Whenever I came into the portacabin at the jail on a Thursday, he'd say, "Hey Gordon, how you doing? How's your week? Have the boys been up to see you?" When he leaves, he always says, "Tell the kids I say hello." He's got the capacity to remember a face and remember something that's important to them.

'Over the weeks we've talked about why I'm inside and my appeal. I've been diagnosed as bipolar and I've had conversations with him about that too. He's been so supportive of me, and I think he gets a lot out of it as well.

'Mental health affects all of us. Blokes don't talk – but they should do. When you talk you fix yourselves quicker. Or you fix somebody else. Just by having a chat.

'He's asked how I cope in the environment that I'm in. It is difficult. You have to be stiff upper lip and one of the lads, all that. If I was sat in that other room with them all right now, I'd try not to be in tears like this. But I'm an emotional person. I'm broken inside. I'm six foot three, but sometimes in prison I feel five foot six. I just don't feel up to lifting my shoulders.

'I go and lock myself in my room no end of times. Sometimes I cry, sometimes I just can't be arsed to go out. I go out, get my dinner, go back. Someone will say, "I haven't seen you for a few days." No, because I didn't feel strong enough to talk to people. Sometimes I don't feel strong enough to put on the masculinity front. That's all Billy bullshit, to be fair. They're all giving it this and that, when the reality is everyone's struggling. They just don't want to admit it.

'I'm going to really miss seeing Jason on a Thursday for the football sessions, but that's coincided with me being afforded more town visits. I've lost something big, but gained something even bigger.

'Whenever I call home I always say, "Doz says hello," and my missus goes, "You don't really know him though, do you?" "Yeah, I do!" And I know he'll be there for me when I get out too. My lad plays youth football and he says he's going to get a few of his mates together so we can start a team I can coach. If I've got this badge I may as well use it. I can't wait.'

I have to admit, I got pretty emotional reading that. Gordon's right, I will be there for him when gets out – 100 per cent. He's not the only one. Certain people didn't give up on me when I'd made mistakes and was at my lowest ebb, now I want to provide that same sort of support for others in a similar position.

I definitely feel I can relate to those guys inside. Sometimes it's just a feeling, isn't it? Some people you just feel you can talk to. When you get the feeling someone is not there to judge then you feel comfortable opening up. When you get that connection, and you feel someone has genuinely got your back, you can just tell.

I know I'm in a good place when I'm not walking around judging anybody. It's incredible what we feel we can judge without walking in somebody's shoes. We sometimes judge to make ourselves feel better – I think it's a thing we do when we're not happy. I started doing it. It's wrong. When you get judged by people who haven't spent one minute in your company it's hard.

Now I'm asking people not to judge me, so I have to give everybody else that courtesy back.

The prison work has been great for me in that regard. It wasn't by design that I've ended up doing it, but perhaps it was fate. It's certainly helped with the healing process.

Writing this book has made it easier for me because I know more about myself now than I ever did. I don't think I could have gone into the prisons before the drug-drive incident and my interview in the paper. No way. I couldn't talk openly to them like I do now.

But I've been on a journey where I've acknowledged my past and taken accountability. There has to be that acknowledgement before you can move forwards. Show a little bit of remorse, say sorry and move forwards. If you don't do that then you can't move on.

I do think I have a skill where I can get people to open up. Maybe further down the line it's something I can get into more.

23

Joining the Dots

ONCE I realised my life hadn't been normal, that's when I became complex. But once I started to understand mental health more, that's when things became a little bit easier.

I had six sessions of counselling, opened up a bit, but it wasn't for me. The guy was a recovering addict and he was always trying to second guess me, saying, 'This is what you're going to do.' I didn't like that.

This book is my therapy. This has been counselling for me. I've not flinched when baring my soul. The only way for me to go forward was to do this. I don't have to bury or hide anything any more. This is it. This is me.

This book was so you could step in my shoes, go through my journey and come to your own conclusion. What that conclusion is won't make any difference to me because I know how I feel. Hopefully though you'll stop and think, 'Wow, there was more to all that than I realised.'

That piece I did in the paper really brought it home. *What's really going on? Where is the problem? Why are you fighting yourself?* I had to go back and try and piece it together.

As I've said so many times, 'I wish it didn't happen, but it did.' I'm now dealing with the consequences of the past. You do something and other stuff's going to happen further down the line. I can't change any of that now. I can reflect on it, though.

Looking back, I was always fighting a personal battle. That's from long before I became a footballer. Everything was always complicated. I've never felt like everyone else. I've always felt different.

I've made mistakes, yes. Some of it is down to society. There's vulnerability in my story. From nought to 16, I was quiet, sheltered, disciplined, made sacrifices. It was only football, no drama. From 16 onwards, things changed.

There's been something missing in my life – that's a fact. As I've said, it was all trial and error. I made so many decisions on my own when I really needed help to make them.

I love my mum to bits, but you need that father figure. Or at least some kind of father figure. Tony wasn't equipped to provide that for me. No one checked on me, not properly anyway. I wish I had what I've given Andre. I never had a phone call the night before a game with someone asking, 'Are you eating properly?' and saying, 'Make sure you get a good night's sleep,' then, after the game, someone checking in to ask, 'How do you think that went?' and to say, 'Don't worry about that.'

I had no boundaries. Out in the park until ten o'clock every night. A 12-year-old going into the North Stand with no adults. You wouldn't get that these days.

The debut goal made me grow up fast. I was thrown into the deep end and had to quickly develop a lot of the social skills

I hadn't acquired growing up. I wasn't ready for that. If you don't know anything about the world, if you can't recognise danger, then you're in trouble. I thought everyone was nice and had my best interests at heart. I was naive.

If you think the professional game is just a case of turning up and playing football on a Saturday then you're wrong. There are so many other things to deal with. *Who are all these people? Why are they trying to be friendly? What do they want? Who is genuine and who is not?* My childhood left me unprepared to face all that at such a young age. The football was OK, it was all the other bits that were the problem.

We can all point fingers, but the bottom line is you've got a 15-year-old kid who was thrust into the professional football world without the tools. Socially he's useless and insecure. Psychologically he's not ready. Now he's starting to drink and it makes him feel different. I think anybody who had the childhood I had would have been the same – I'm sure they would. I'm just being honest here. If people don't get it, they don't get it. I had to get all this out, though.

I'm not playing my violin. I know I'm lucky to have had the career I've had. I wouldn't change it for the world. I'm just trying to figure it all out. Am I making excuses for the way I behaved? Am I actually that person? That's what I've got to uncover. I haven't got a choirboy's record, but I'd like to think I've got the heart and decency of a human being.

I was a kid with a talent and nothing else. The football pitch was my sanctuary. But the debut goal brought attention and that side of it was a struggle. *Why me? Why has this happened like this?* Everything happens so quick. You blink and your career is over. It's been great for me talking about all this. I've had to go all the way back.

How did it affect me not having a dad growing up? The consequences of that were maybe found out as I got older. You can't dwell on things for ever, though. The past is the past. Sometimes you end up paying for the past for a long time. That's what's happened to me. I'll probably be paying for the past for ever. I've just got to handle it better. I'm comfortable with that.

The whole nature/nurture debate is an interesting one for me. Am I the way I am because of my genes or my upbringing? My dad loves to party, and my mum's had her fair share of chaos, but I don't think my life was by design. I was shaped by events. The debut goal was always going to change me. I can't lie, the attention was great – it really was. I wouldn't change it, but now I'm a lot older and wiser, and I know more about myself, I realise I wasn't ready for all that.

Sometimes I do feel a bit of a prisoner to the debut goal story. When you do something that monstrous in your first game your career becomes for ever associated with that moment. How would my life have played out without that goal? That's a great question. Less early pressure and attention might have helped. Then again, maybe everything else doesn't follow without it?

I'm still the youngest ever goalscorer in English top-flight history. I do get annoyed when they just mention the Premier League era. I think it's a little bit disrespectful to all the ones who played before. The ones who set the true records don't really get a shout, do they? It's always 'the youngest Premier

League goalscorer' when they talk about it on the TV. But I beat all of them by a distance. I know that. My mum knows. Ipswich fans know. That's what matters.

It wasn't like I was 16, nearly 17 when I scored that goal. I had just got past 15. Sixteen years and 57 days old. I was a child. I don't think that record will ever be broken. I don't think it can be broken. A schoolkid playing in the Premier League, where they are all mentally tuned-in athletes now. I might be wrong, but I just can't see it.

In April 2009, Connor Wickham made his debut for Ipswich, aged 16 years and 11 days, in a 3-1 home defeat against Doncaster Rovers. That saw him beat my record as the club's youngest ever player by 46 days. It wasn't in the top flight though and he didn't score, so he can have that one!

In September 2022, Arsenal brought Ethan Nwaneri on in the 89th minute of a Premier League win at Brentford. Aged 15 years and 181 days, he became the youngest ever player to appear in the top flight of English football. He hasn't been seen since, though. Why did he get his debut? Because Chelsea were after him. Arsenal played him to keep him happy and he signed a new contract. Call me cynical but that's how I see it. I know how this game works. If my record had got broken because of something like that, I would have been after Mikel Arteta, I can tell you!

Saturday, 4 February 2023 marked the 40th anniversary of my debut goal. There aren't many records that stand that long. I'm in the history books. I just hope and pray I stay there.

Should I have stayed at Ipswich in 1993? Could I have been a one-club man? They are really tough questions to answer. The move to Tottenham happened so quick. If I'd had someone to talk to, maybe I would have stayed. I don't know. If I'm honest, thinking about it, I probably would have still gone. There was a grand a week more on the table. I liked nice things. I can't lie and say that wasn't part of it. Tottenham were my second team and they're a big, big club. Sometimes you have to take these opportunities because they might not happen again. Andre turned down Liverpool at a young age to stay at Ipswich and things didn't work out the way he hoped they would. Hindsight's a wonderful thing.

Would my life have been less chaotic had I not gone to Spurs? London is certainly a different place to Ipswich. That said, there would still have been distractions for me. I was going to London a lot when I was at Ipswich anyway. In theory it sounds great, getting 600, 700 games for Ipswich, but it might not have worked out that way. There's no point dwelling on that particular 'what if?'

I played in the early years of the Premier League, but it was after I finished when the finances really boomed. When I played the wages were steady year after year. They were at a level that people on the street could still almost relate to. But then – boom! – it just went nuts. The Bosman ruling came in 1995 and that played its part. When I was on four and a half grand a week in the mid-'90s, I never thought there would be a 50-grand-a-week footballer. Now there are players supposedly on 200 grand a week. They call me 'Lucky Jim'!

Joking aside, I don't look at that as a missed opportunity at all. To be honest, I'd probably be dead if I'd earned that sort of money! Seriously, I think it would have caused me drama the way I was. More money, more problems. I always used to look back at the Ipswich '81 side and think about what they got compared to my generation. I've always tried to be one of those guys who is happy with what he's got.

I wasn't the biggest saver during my career. I invested in pensions and some property, but in 2008, thanks to a combination of the recession and a divorce, I lost a few quid. Money soon goes. I've got a place in Cape Verde which I'm waiting to cash in on, but that's all I've got at the minute. I'm not in debt, but I'm not wealthy either. At the end of the day, if I really needed to, I could call upon Andre. He has helped me in the past and I'm very grateful for that.

Another question I get asked is how I think I'd fare, in my prime, in today's game. I have to say, I'd back myself. Technically, my game might have been appreciated more and utilised better away from an era of 4-4-2. Everyone plays with at least one number ten in the pocket now, many teams with two. True, the game is quicker and more physical now, but I think I would have adapted to that. Players don't drink these days, so it's unlikely I would have been drawn into that culture. I'd be fitter than I was thanks to the advancements in sports science. My rhythm would be the same as everyone else's.

Putting together this book has reminded me that I'm ninth in the list of all-time appearance-makers for Ipswich Town (414 games) and tenth in the all-time top scorers list (73 goals). I was captain when the club got promoted too. What does that mean? It means I made a mark. A skinny little kid from Elliott Street, who grew up a few hundred yards from the stadium, has made a big mark at his hometown club that he supported fanatically. That's *Roy of the Rovers* stuff, really, isn't it? Write it as a piece of fiction and it would probably be dismissed as too fanciful.

In 2015, I was inducted into the Ipswich Town Hall of Fame. To be in there with so many legends – my heroes – is something I still have to pinch myself about. I received that recognition at Portman Road, fittingly, alongside the man who started it all for me – Bobby Ferguson. That night, I just kept thinking, 'How the hell have you done this?'

Recently, I took part in a Q&A evening with some former team-mates. An audience member asked, 'Who's the best player you ever played with?' Kevin Wilson said, 'Jason Dozzell.' Gavin Johnson said, 'Jason Dozzell.' That took me aback. Hearing things like that is exactly what I've been missing. What's so hard in saying nice things like that? Why don't others around me say that to me more? The people I'm surrounded by are just not tapped into me and what makes me tick. Sadly, I've been surrounded by a lot of negativity and often I allow those negative thoughts to swallow up all the positive stuff. When I talk about the things I've achieved it makes me feel good. Do I get enough of that? No. Now I know I need to be hanging around with positive people, not negative ones.

Another thing I got asked at that Q&A night was, 'Who was your mentor?' That also stopped me in my tracks. I couldn't give an answer. In the end I had to say 'myself'. That made me go away and reflect. I've had people who have supported me, as you've read, but never one ever-present voice of reason and guiding hand.

Could I have had a bigger career without those blow-out summers and off-field drama? Possibly. There was definitely a long period in my life when I didn't like how things had turned out. But now I've connected a lot of the dots and come to the conclusion that maybe I achieved more than I should have. I don't care what other people think looking in from the outside. Given the cards I was dealt, I did really well. That's the way I'm looking at it.

Life is calmer for me now. I'm finding ways to be comfortable with the middle ground. I don't want to hurt anybody, I don't want to bring strife to anybody, I don't want to get into any trouble. I just want to be there for my kids, my mum, my family and my girlfriend. I'm even a granddad now. I love being a granddad, I just hate that bloody word!

My job at the Ipswich Town Foundation really helps. I'm a coach on the Football and Education Programme that has several boys' and girls' teams, all aged 16 to 18. My son Emile is on it. It means I'm on the practice pitch at Portman Road five days a week and that's really, really good for me mentally. I go to my mum's every day for lunch and make that same walk to the ground as I did as a kid. Every single time I take those steps all those good childhood memories come flooding back – watching the '81 team train, waiting for the ball to come over, playing on that park until ten o'clock. It brings all the good out of me. For me to be happy, I need to be near that special place. That area is still my sanctuary.

After the court case in 2019 I had a plan. I thought, 'I'm changing my life, I don't need any more stress.' I don't think I'm that strong mentally – I'm actually quite fragile – but I knew I had to deal with my head better than I had done. When things aren't right, when I'm feeling a bit edgy, I've got to deal with it better than I did or else I'll be back where I was.

I live on my own, but I have a lovely girlfriend, Tracy, who I see every day without fail. I've told her everything and let her into why I am the way I am. She knows what signs to look out for. I still have bad days, of course I do, but I can control them better. I speak to Milts too if I feel myself going a certain way, whereas before I would bury it all deep. At least now I know what a bad day looks like. Before I didn't even realise I was having one.

Forward planning is a big thing. I'll think, 'OK, I've got a couple of free days coming up here,' and make sure I fill one of them to avoid those triggers of boredom and time on my hands. It's all about keeping busy. I can cope with the odd day on my own if I know the next day I'm doing something. It's nice to be on your own now and again. That shows me I'm making progress because I couldn't ever be on my own before.

In the interview I did after my court case, I said, 'I've had enough nights out in my life. If I never have another night out again, I'll have still had enough for a lifetime,' and added that I wanted '20–30 years stress-free'. I meant all of it.

I don't want to be that old man who's out drinking all the time. Emile's 18 now and out with his mates. I'll leave that to them. If I go out it's the pub and home by midnight. Anything after that scares me. It turns into something stupid. Two o'clock comes around and panic sets in. When that happens, I ain't going home. That can't happen any more. I'm not perfect, but I'm trying. That's all I can say.

The meaning behind the title of this book, *Follow the Thunder*, hopefully became apparent on the very first page. As a young child I heard that burst of noise and soon became drawn to it. Putting that electricity in the air myself was a thrill. Away from the football field, I always felt a magnetic pull towards stormy weather too. For a long time, I found comfort in that chaos. Now, finally, it's time for the clouds to break.

Acknowledgements

This is my chance to reiterate a few thank yous.

To Mum – you're the number one person in my life and always will be.

To Dion, Andre and Emile – I'm in awe of the men you've grown to be. Thank you for all your support.

To Leonie – you did the hard yards with our children and made them the fantastic people they are.

To Dad – that hug transformed me. I wish we'd had it sooner.

To Roy Knightsbridge – 'Super Sundays' were among the happiest times of my life. You were a father figure to me when I needed one.

To Tony Dable – without you stepping in, I might not have been an Ipswich player.

To Bobby Ferguson – gone but never forgotten. You gave me the chance to do something monstrous.

To Terry Butcher and Russell Osman – I loved the way you looked after me as a kid and I love the way you still look after me now. Legends.

To Simon Milton – your intervention was truly life-changing. I'll never forget that.

To Pasquale Iachetta and Dennis Tennial – sorry for losing track of who my real friends are. You were there when it mattered.

To Horry Money – for your legal assistance leading up to the court case.

To Cathy – after all the hassle I gave you, you were still so supportive.

To Ipswich Town Football Club – you didn't have to give me a second chance, but you did. For that I'll always be grateful. My current job means the world to me.

To Tracy – you are helping to make me a better person.